# Personal Investment Journal

by b<sup>pro</sup>ookmark™

---◇═══◆═══◇---

A stock market research guide for the
frustrated individual investor who
Cannot follow the cryptic methods of
gurus, Does not have a super computer
in the basement, and Cannot spend 10
hours a day studying the market

## Dr. Roger D. Smith

*Personal Investment Journal by ProBookmark™: A stock market research guide for the frustrated individual investor who Cannot follow the cryptic methods of gurus, Does not have a super computer in the basement, and Cannot spend 10 hours a day studying the market*

Modelbenders Press books may be purchased for business and promotional use or for special sales. For information please contact the publisher.

ProBookmark™ is a trademark of Modelbenders LLC.

PRINTED IN THE UNITED STATES OF AMERICA

Visit our web site at www.modelbenders.com

Designed by Adina Cucicov at Flamingo Designs
Cover image: © Vivian Seefeld—Fotolia.com

The Library of Congress has cataloged the paperback edition as follows:

Smith, Roger
    Personal Investment Journal by ProBookmark™: A stock market research guide for the frustrated individual investor who Cannot follow the cryptic methods of gurus, Does not have a super computer in the basement, and Cannot spend 10 hours a day studying the market. Roger Smith. – 1st ed.
    1. Business & Economics: Investments & Securities–Stocks
    2. Business & Economics: Personal Finance–Investing
    3. Education: Finance
    I. Roger Smith   II. Title

ISBN 978-0-9843993-8-3

## ProBookmark™ Series

*ProBookmark™:*
*Capturing the riches you read for a lifetime*

*ProBookmark™ for Bible Study:*
*Capturing your study of the Bible for a lifetime*

*Daily Goals Journal by ProBookmark™:*
*Achieving your goals through daily action*

*Night Mind™ by ProBookmark™:*
*Capturing the wisdom of your sleeping mind*

*Project Management Journal by ProBookmark™:*
*Graphically tracking projects, tasks, and performance*

*Personal Investment Journal by ProBookmark™*

# Personal Investment Journal
## by ProBookmark™

*How much time do you put into each investment decision?*

*Are you simply reacting to the advice you see on television?*

*Do you know what a company does before you invest in it?*

*Do you know how the company and the stock have performed over the past year or ten years?*

Most individual investors would have to answer "No" to all of these questions. Some do not research a stock because they do not want to take the time. Some have no idea where to get the information. Others do not know what to do with the information even when they are looking at it on the screen.

This *Personal Investment Journal* will help you overcome all of these problems in investing.

1) We will show you where to get relevant information about a company.
2) We will give you a quick method for analyzing that information.
3) We will help you get through this in an organized and efficient manner.

Making the final investment decision will be up to you.

Personal Investment Journal
by bookmark™

Throughout my investment career I have read dozens of books
on how to think about investing, how to analyze companies, and
how to buy and sell stocks. All of those were helpful. But all of
them shared a common problem. They presented a set of equa-
tions that I was not able to work through every time I was interested in an investment. They called for data that I was not able
to find on investing web sites.

This Journal is different. Every piece of data on the Stock Tracker is readily available from the major financial web sites. This
Journal takes advantage of all of the in-depth calculations that
have already done by those web sites. We are not asking you to
repeat the detailed work that professional financial analysts have
already done and posted on the web.

Before you buy or sell a stock, you need to open this book and
spend 10 to 20 minutes working through a two page analysis of
the stock. This will put more data about the company and the
investment in your hands than almost all amateur investors use
when making a decision.

The *Personal Investment Journal* does not contain any secret for-
mulas that will tell you what will happen to a company or a stock
in the future. The Journal just organizes important information
that any disciplined and serious investor should be considering.

The analysis that you will do in this Journal is similar to what the professionals do before making an investment. In fact, you will be taking advantage of the work that hundreds of professionals have already done for you. Once you have a more complete picture of the stock and the company, you will be in a much better position to make your own decision about whether an investment is right for you.

The Journal will also become a personal history book. Looking back through past decisions you will begin to see a pattern in your own investments. You will see the good and bad investment decisions that you have made in the past, which is the beginning of building a more successful approach.

You can combine this Journal with any of the hundreds of other investment books out there. Those books may suggest specific calculations and thresholds for making a decision. This Journal is where you collect the information that paints a portrait of the company you are interested in. This is where you get your first sense of whether you are looking at a beautiful or an ugly company.

Don't make another investment decision without first collecting and analyzing the essential information about the company and the stock you are buying. The *Personal Investment Journal* is your personal tool for doing this.

## Data Sources

The information necessary to complete a Stock Tracker can be found many different places on the Internet. If you use an online stock brokerage account it probably contains almost all of this information, including their own tools for analyzing that information. The information is also available freely on web sites like:

- www.MSN.com
- www.Yahoo.com
- www.Google.com
- www.Stockpickr.com
- www.Zacks.com
- www.GuruFocus.com
- www.SeekingAlpha.com

All of these sites have access to the same data and they have a small army of employees who decide how best to organize and present it on their web site. If you do not already have a favorite effective tool for data analysis, then you may want to look at each of these to see the different emphases that they place on specific types of data.

For the *Personal Investment Journal* we have structured the forms around the data on the "www.MSN.com/money" web site. This site is a very rich source that is well organized and easy to navigate. But, each of the sites listed above have at least one feature that is better than its competitors. So you may want to look at several of them to find your favorite and to get a different perspective on the data.

# How to use the Personal Investment Journal by ProBookmark™

When analyzing a stock, you are primarily trying to determine two things.

1) Is the company a good solid performer that is expected to grow bigger, richer, and stronger in the coming years?

2) If it is a good company, then what is a fair price to pay for a share of the stock?

There is actually a third question that everyone in the world wishes they could answer.

3) Will the stock appreciate in value shortly after I purchase it?

Answering that third question requires special powers of ESP, telepathy, and fortune telling. But, it is exactly what very smart and very well paid people on Wall Street attempt to do all day, every day.

Individual investors have no chance of beating these professionals at their mystical game of fortune telling. Each of us is usually working alone, without a super-computer in our basement, and with very limited cash to risk on new ideas.

Your goal as an individual investor is to pay a fair price for a great company and then enjoy the inevitable success of that company over many years. You cannot out-guess the professionals in predicting the short term movements of the stock. That is a fool's game.

The Stock Trackers in this book present two views of an investment. The first view is based on information about the stock. The second is based on information about the company. Together these will help you decide whether you want to invest your hard-earned money in the company and at what price.

The Stock Trackers cannot tell you what to do. They paint a picture which you will have to evaluate yourself and make your own decisions. We just want these to be informed and educated decisions before you invest your money.

The stock market is not a casino or a race track. You should not be placing your money on wild hunches or whispered tips. You should be buying solid companies at fair prices, preferably bargain prices.

## Stock Tracker

1. **Company, Symbol, Date.** Enter the name of the company, its stock symbol, and the date on which you are doing the analysis. Like all good Journals, this is the header that you will use it to refer back to past decisions and lessons learned.

2. **Attention Trigger.** Why are you thinking about this stock? What brought it to your attention? When you write this trigger down, you will often realize that your interest is based on very thin or sketchy information.

3. **Graph.** A one year graph of the ups and down of the stock can tell you how wild a ride the stock can give you. Can you stand to be on this ride? The graph should lead you to ask whether the stock can continue performing as it has for the last year.
   a. Select a "1 year" period for the graph.
   b. Click the "Compare" button and choose one of the indices for comparison.
   c. The left end of the graph is one year in the past and will show both the stock and the index at "0". Then there will be a steady progression as the two lines stagger above and below that beginning level through the next year.
   d. The right end of the graph will show the percentage that the stock and the index have changed over the year.
   e. Take a minute to roughly sketch the stock curve on the page. If the stock is up significantly over the last year, then why you believe that it will go up even higher? If

it is down, then why do you think it might turn around and head up now? Finally, if it has been flat for a year, then why do you believe it is about to perform better than it has in the past? All of these are very common sense questions that too few people ask about their investments before they throw their money in.

4. **Quote/Financial Highlights.** The "Financial Highlights" section of the web site provides the most basic information about the stock.
   a. **Stock Price.** What price is the stock trading at right now?
   b. **EPS.** What were the Earnings Per Share in the last reported year?
   c. **P/E.** The ratio between the Price and the EPS is the first number divided by the second. Traditionally, a P/E below 10 has been considered a bargain or a company that is failing. A P/E above 20 has been considered overpriced or a company that everyone believes will grow explosively. A P/E between 10 and 20 is common for most stocks and may not clearly indicate what the market expects in the future.
   d. **Market Cap.** The total value of all of the stock of the company. This tells you whether you are dealing with a small company in the millions, a medium sized company in the 100's of millions to low billions, or a large company over 10 billion dollars.
   e. **Div (Yield).** The quarterly dividend that the company pays to shareholders, and the percent annual return (yield), which this represents. Compare the Yields of

several different companies, as well as the yield from a bond or CD.

f. **Debt/Equity.** How much debt does this company have with respect to the total equity? Like an individual, a company that has more debt than equity should have a good reason for borrowing so much money.

g. **EPS Growth.** In the last year, how many months had an EPS Growth that was Positive (Pos) and how many Negative (Neg)?

5. **10 Year Summary.** There is a wealth of data about the historical performance of this company. In this section you are just counting the number of years that it had a Positive change (Pos) and a Negative change (Neg).

a. **EBIT.** Earnings Before Interest and Taxes is a popular way of measuring the real profits of a company. A growing company usually has more earnings each year, with a few down years.

b. **Assets.** The estimated value of all of the things that the company owns, such as cash, factories, trucks, inventory, and equipment. In most cases, assets should be increasing if the company is growing.

c. **LT Debt.** All companies borrow money to operate, which causes them to incur Long Term Debt. But they should have a cycle of borrowing and then paying this money back, not digging themselves deeper into debt every year.

6. **Value Price.** Warren Buffet and his army of followers emphasize that the key to a profitable investment is simply purchasing it at a fair price in the beginning. Three potential bargain prices are included here. Compare these to the current Stock Price to get a feel for whether this stock is trading at a good price.

    a. **EPS*10.** Simply take the EPS number in the left-hand column and add a zero. Stocks trading at 10 times EPS or less are often considered a bargain.

    b. **EPS*15.** Multiply the EPS times 15. Finding a good company at ten-times EPS is tough, but finding one at 15 times is much more likely.

    c. **Book/Share.** The Book Value per Share can be found on the web site. It indicates the value of the company if it were liquidated, the debts paid, and the remaining money divided up among the shareholders. Historically, this was considered the real value of a share of the company. But, today value is based more on expected earnings growth.

7. **Key Ratios.** Financial ratios slice and dice a company in dozens of different ways. Each ratio illustrates a unique value of the company. Financial web sites provide the average ratios for the entire industry. These are a great way to compare your stock idea to its competitors. There are so many different ratios that they are found on sub-pages under the "Key Ratio" section. In the Stock Tracker, "G" identifies those on the "Growth" page; "P" on the "Price Ratio" page; "M" on the "Profit Margin" page; and "I" on the "Investment Return" page.

a. **G: Sales.** Growth rate of the company's sales. How does that compare to the entire industry? Is this company growing faster than the rest of the industry? If it is not, then which company is the leader in growth?

b. **G: Income.** What is the growth rate of the company's income?

c. **P: Price/Sales.** The Price-to-Sales ratio is similar to the P/E in that it compares the stock price to the money coming in via sales.

d. **P: Price/Book.** The stock price divided by the Book Value per Share compares the price to the value you could get if everything in the company were sold off and you received the cash.

e. **P: Price/CF.** Compares the price to the Cash Flow of the company.

f. **M: Net.** Net Margin is the percentage profit margins that the company is generating.

g. **I: ROE.** Percentage Return on Equity in the company.

h. **I: ROA.** Percentage Return on Assets of the company.

i. **I: ROC.** Percentage Return on Capital.

8. **Personal Call.** Once you have finished both sides of the Stock Tracker form, return here and enter your own opinions on whether this seems to be a good company that is trading at a fair price.

a. **Price.** Is this company trading at a Bargain, Fair, High, or Crazy price?

b. **Decision.** Should you Buy, Wait, or Ignore this stock?

(Back of Form)

9. **Industry and Leader.** Identify the industry that this company is part of, as well as the leader in that industry. Know who the competition is and consider whether you are making the best investment in this industry.

10 **Key Ratios: 10 Year Summary.** Create a simple picture of the ten year performance of the company in a number of different areas. Enter the ratio for the company ten years ago and that for the most current year. Does the company appear to be in a better position now than it was 10 years ago?

11. **Analyst Ratings.** Most companies have a number of professional analysts that are dedicated to studying their performance and publishing an opinion. These analysts do more research on the company than you will ever be able to match. Look at these professionals' opinion of the stock's future prospects. They usually assign a rating of *Strong Buy, Moderate Buy, Hold, Moderate Sell, or Strong Sell.* On Wall Street these opinions are often seen as overly optimistic. So a vote to "Hold" is often interpreted as meaning "Sell". A vote to "Sell" suggests that every professional has already sold out their position.

12. **SEC Filings.** Publicly traded companies must submit key financial documents to the Securities and Exchange Commission. All of these are public record and you can find links to them on this page. The 10K is an annual financial state-

ment with details about the company's operations. The 10Q is a quarterly financial statement. Since buying a stock is like investing in a marriage you should know intimate details about the company.

 a. **CEO.** Who is the CEO? How long have they been there? What did they do before?

 b. **CFO.** Same questions for the person in charge of the money.

 c. **Rational.** In their letter to shareholders do they sound like rational people with a real plan for making the company successful? Can you make sense of what they are saying? Do you believe it? If you can't understand and swallow their story then why would you trust them with your money?

 d. **Moat Size.** What makes their business difficult to copy? Would it be easy for another company to duplicate everything they have done, or would that be very difficult?

 e. **New Products.** What new products have they created recently? Have they acquired another company? Both of these tell you something about their future plans.

 f. **Competitive Advantage.** What advantage does this company have over every other company in its industry? Why can they be more successful than others?

 g. **Profit Engine.** What will cause their profits to grow? If the profits do not grow larger, the stock price will not go higher.

13. **Research.** Do some reading on major financial web sites to learn about the company, its history, its philosophy, its repu-

tation, and what it tells the media about its future plans. The Stock Tracker lists six very valuable sites. You may have your own favorites to add to the list.

## Repeat

This *Personal Investment Journal by ProBookmark*™ contains 50 Stock Tracker forms, along with several recurring stock summaries. If you use this tool regularly you will fill the book quickly with your ideas and analyses. When the first book is full, it is time to get another one and keep growing. After a few years you will have an entire set of these, each filled with valuable insights into your own style, performance, and learning curve. These are the records of your victories, failures, and lessons learned. They will put you in a position to improve your performance, which is something that most investors never do.

Use this journal to build your expertise and improve your long-term profits.

Best Wishes,
**Roger Smith**

# Stocks of Interest

Personal Investment Journal
by bookmark™

1 ...............................................................................................................................

..................................................................................................................................

2 ...............................................................................................................................

..................................................................................................................................

3 ...............................................................................................................................

..................................................................................................................................

4 ...............................................................................................................................

..................................................................................................................................

5 ...............................................................................................................................

..................................................................................................................................

6 ...............................................................................................................................

..................................................................................................................................

7 ...............................................................................................................................

..................................................................................................................................

8 ...............................................................................................................................

..................................................................................................................................

9 ...............................................................................................................................

..................................................................................................................................

10 .............................................................................................................................

..................................................................................................................................

11 .............................................................................................................................

..................................................................................................................................

12 .............................................................................................................................

..................................................................................................................................

# Stocks of Interest

13 ...................................................................................................................................

..........................................................................................................................................

14 ...................................................................................................................................

..........................................................................................................................................

15 ...................................................................................................................................

..........................................................................................................................................

16 ...................................................................................................................................

..........................................................................................................................................

17 ...................................................................................................................................

..........................................................................................................................................

18 ...................................................................................................................................

..........................................................................................................................................

19 ...................................................................................................................................

..........................................................................................................................................

20 ...................................................................................................................................

..........................................................................................................................................

21 ...................................................................................................................................

..........................................................................................................................................

22 ...................................................................................................................................

..........................................................................................................................................

23 ...................................................................................................................................

..........................................................................................................................................

24 ...................................................................................................................................

..........................................................................................................................................

# Stock Tracker

company ............................................................... symbol .......... date ..............

attention trigger ........................................................................................

................................................................................................................

## graph (1 year)

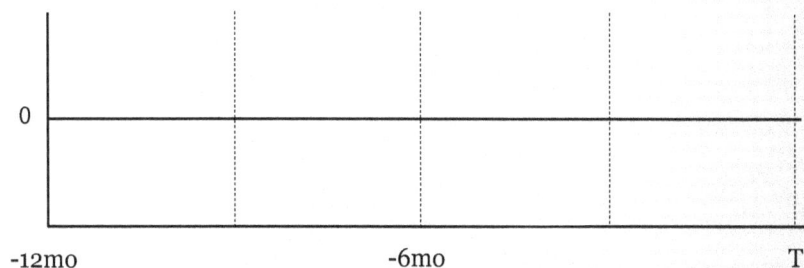

0 _____

-12mo                    -6mo                              T

## quote/financial highlights

Stock Price: _____

EPS: _____

P/E: _____

Market Cap: _____

Div (Yield): _____

Debt/Equity: _____

EPS Growth: Pos ____ Neg ____

## quote/financial highlights

EBIT:        Pos ____ Neg ____

Assets:      Pos ____ Neg ____

LT Debt:     Pos ____ Neg ____

## value price

EPS*10:      _____

EPS*15:      _____

Book/Share: _____

## key ratios

| | Company | Industry |
|---|---|---|
| SG: Sales | _____ | _____ |
| G: Income | _____ | _____ |
| P: Price/Sales | _____ | _____ |
| P: Price/Book | _____ | _____ |
| P: Price/CF | _____ | _____ |
| M: Net | _____ | _____ |
| I: ROE | _____ | _____ |
| I: ROA | _____ | _____ |
| I: ROC | _____ | _____ |

## personal call

price | bargain | fair | high | crazy |   decision | buy | wait | ignore

# Stock Tracker

company .................................................................................................

industry ........................................... industry leader .................................

## key ratios: 10 yr comparisons

P/E: _____ > _____
P/S: _____ > _____
P/B: _____ > _____
Net Profit: _____ > _____
Book/Share: _____ > _____
ROE: _____ > _____
ROA: _____ > _____

## analyst ratings

| Strong Buy | | | Mod Buy |
|---|---|---|---|
| | Hold | | |
| Strong Sell | | | Mod Sell |
| | Buy | Sell | |
| Insiders | | | |

## sec filings (10K/10Q)

CEO: Name _____ Years _____ Prior _____
CFO: Name _____ Years _____ Prior _____
Rational: _____ Moat Size: _____
New Products or Acquisitions: _____
_____
Competitive Advantage: _____
_____
_____
Profit Engine: _____
_____

## research

Company Web Site: _____
Wikipedia.org: _____
Google News: _____
CNBC.com: _____
Fortune.com: _____
BusinessWeek.com: _____

# Stock Tracker

Personal Investment Journal
by bookmark™

company ............................................................ symbol ......... date ...............

attention trigger ..........................................................................................

..........................................................................................................................

### graph (1 year)

```
0 ├──────────────────────────────────────────
  │
  └──────────────────────────────────────────
  -12mo              -6mo                    T
```

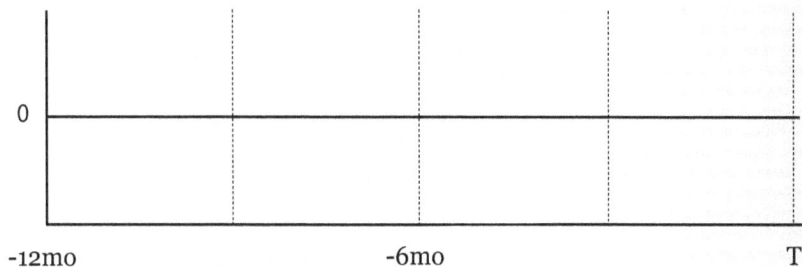

### quote/financial highlights

Stock Price: _____
EPS: _____
P/E: _____
Market Cap: _____
Div (Yield): _____
Debt/Equity: _____
EPS Growth: Pos ____ Neg ____

### quote/financial highlights

EBIT: Pos ____ Neg ____
Assets: Pos ____ Neg ____
LT Debt: Pos ____ Neg ____

### value price

EPS*10: _____
EPS*15: _____
Book/Share: _____

| key ratios | Company | Industry |
|---|---|---|
| SG: Sales | _____ | _____ |
| G: Income | _____ | _____ |
| P: Price/Sales | _____ | _____ |
| P: Price/Book | _____ | _____ |
| P: Price/CF | _____ | _____ |
| M: Net | _____ | _____ |
| I: ROE | _____ | _____ |
| I: ROA | _____ | _____ |
| I: ROC | _____ | _____ |

### personal call

| price | bargain | fair | high | crazy | decision | buy | wait | ignore |
|---|---|---|---|---|---|---|---|---|

# Stock Tracker

company ................................................................................................

industry .................................. industry leader ................................

---

## key ratios: 10 yr comparisons

P/E: _____ > _____
P/S: _____ > _____
P/B: _____ > _____
Net Profit: _____ > _____
Book/Share: _____ > _____
ROE: _____ > _____
ROA: _____ > _____

## analyst ratings

| Strong Buy | | | Mod Buy |
| Hold | | | |
| Strong Sell | | | Mod Sell |
| Insiders | Buy | Sell | |

---

## sec filings (10K/10Q)

CEO: Name _____ Years _____ Prior _____
CFO: Name _____ Years _____ Prior _____
Rational: _____ Moat Size: _____
New Products or Acquisitions: _____
_____
Competitive Advantage: _____
_____
_____
Profit Engine: _____
_____

---

## research

Company Web Site: _____
Wikipedia.org: _____
Google News: _____
CNBC.com: _____
Fortune.com: _____
BusinessWeek.com: _____

# Stock Tracker

company ........................................................ symbol ........ date ...............

attention trigger ...................................................................................

........................................................................................................

---

## graph (1 year)

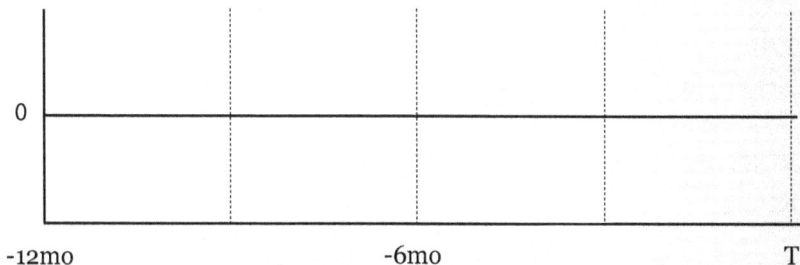

0

-12mo         -6mo         T

---

## quote/financial highlights

Stock Price: _____
EPS: _____
P/E: _____
Market Cap: _____
Div (Yield): _____
Debt/Equity: _____
EPS Growth: Pos ____ Neg ____

## quote/financial highlights

EBIT:     Pos ____ Neg ____
Assets:    Pos ____ Neg ____
LT Debt:   Pos ____ Neg ____

## value price

EPS*10:     _____
EPS*15:     _____
Book/Share: _____

## key ratios

| | Company | Industry |
|---|---|---|
| SG: Sales | _____ | _____ |
| G: Income | _____ | _____ |
| P: Price/Sales | _____ | _____ |
| P: Price/Book | _____ | _____ |
| P: Price/CF | _____ | _____ |
| M: Net | _____ | _____ |
| I: ROE | _____ | _____ |
| I: ROA | _____ | _____ |
| I: ROC | _____ | _____ |

---

## personal call

| price | bargain | fair | high | crazy | decision | buy | wait | ignore |
|---|---|---|---|---|---|---|---|---|

# Stock Tracker

company .......................................................................................................

industry ................................... industry leader ...............................

## key ratios: 10 yr comparisons

P/E:          _____ > _____
P/S:          _____ > _____
P/B:          _____ > _____
Net Profit:   _____ > _____
Book/Share: _____ > _____
ROE:          _____ > _____
ROA:          _____ > _____

## analyst ratings

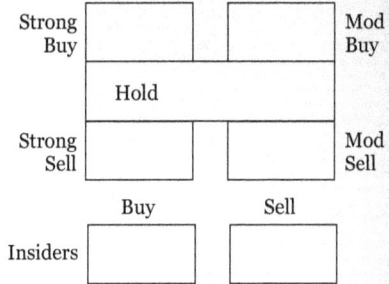

Strong Buy        Mod Buy

Hold

Strong Sell       Mod Sell

Buy        Sell

Insiders

## sec filings (10K/10Q)

CEO: Name _____ Years _____ Prior _____
CFO: Name _____ Years _____ Prior _____
Rational: _____ Moat Size: _____
New Products or Acquisitions: _____
_____
Competitive Advantage: _____
_____
_____
Profit Engine: _____
_____

## research

Company Web Site: _____
Wikipedia.org:      _____
Google News:       _____
CNBC.com:          _____
Fortune.com:       _____

BusinessWeek.com: _____

# Stock Tracker

company ............................................................... symbol .......... date ...............

attention trigger ........................................................................................

....................................................................................................................

## graph (1 year)

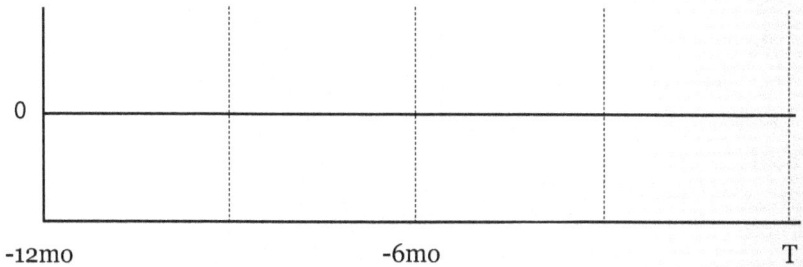

0

-12mo        -6mo        T

## quote/financial highlights

Stock Price: _____

EPS: _____

P/E: _____

Market Cap: _____

Div (Yield): _____

Debt/Equity: _____

EPS Growth: Pos ___ Neg ___

## value price

EPS*10: _____

EPS*15: _____

Book/Share: _____

## key ratios

| | Company | Industry |
|---|---|---|
| SG: Sales | _____ | _____ |
| G: Income | _____ | _____ |
| P: Price/Sales | _____ | _____ |
| P: Price/Book | _____ | _____ |
| P: Price/CF | _____ | _____ |
| M: Net | _____ | _____ |
| I: ROE | _____ | _____ |
| I: ROA | _____ | _____ |
| I: ROC | _____ | _____ |

## quote/financial highlights

EBIT: Pos ___ Neg ___

Assets: Pos ___ Neg ___

LT Debt: Pos ___ Neg ___

## personal call

price | bargain | fair | high | crazy    decision | buy | wait | ignore

# Stock Tracker

Personal Investment Journal
by bookmark™

company ...................................................................................................................

industry .......................................... industry leader .........................................

## key ratios: 10 yr comparisons

P/E:          _____ > _____
P/S:          _____ > _____
P/B:          _____ > _____
Net Profit:   _____ > _____
Book/Share:  _____ > _____
ROE:          _____ > _____
ROA:          _____ > _____

## analyst ratings

| Strong Buy | | Mod Buy |
|---|---|---|
| | Hold | |
| Strong Sell | | Mod Sell |
| | Buy | Sell |
| Insiders | | |

## sec filings (10K/10Q)

CEO: Name _____ Years _____ Prior _____
CFO: Name _____ Years _____ Prior _____
Rational: _____ Moat Size: _____
New Products or Acquisitions: _____
_____
Competitive Advantage: _____
_____
_____
Profit Engine: _____
_____

## research

Company Web Site: _____
Wikipedia.org: _____
Google News: _____
CNBC.com: _____
Fortune.com: _____
BusinessWeek.com: _____

# Stock Tracker

Personal Investment Journal
by bookmark™ [pro]

company ................................................................ symbol ......... date ...............

attention trigger ............................................................................

........................................................................................................

---

## graph (1 year)

0 ├─────────────────────────────────────────────

-12mo                        -6mo                        T

---

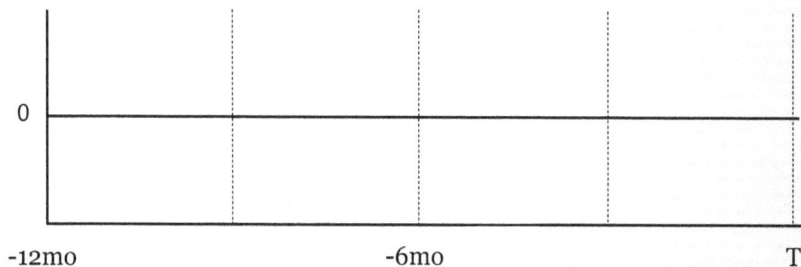

## quote/financial highlights

Stock Price: _____
EPS: _____
P/E: _____
Market Cap: _____
Div (Yield): _____
Debt/Equity: _____
EPS Growth: Pos ____ Neg ____

## quote/financial highlights

EBIT:     Pos ____ Neg ____
Assets:   Pos ____ Neg ____
LT Debt:  Pos ____ Neg ____

## value price

EPS*10: _____
EPS*15: _____
Book/Share: _____

## key ratios

| | Company | Industry |
|---|---|---|
| SG: Sales | _____ | _____ |
| G: Income | _____ | _____ |
| P: Price/Sales | _____ | _____ |
| P: Price/Book | _____ | _____ |
| P: Price/CF | _____ | _____ |
| M: Net | _____ | _____ |
| I: ROE | _____ | _____ |
| I: ROA | _____ | _____ |
| I: ROC | _____ | _____ |

---

## personal call

| price | bargain | fair | high | crazy | decision | buy | wait | ignore |
|---|---|---|---|---|---|---|---|---|

# Stock Tracker

company .......................................................................................................................

industry ........................................... industry leader ..........................................

## key ratios: 10 yr comparisons

P/E: _____ > _____
P/S: _____ > _____
P/B: _____ > _____
Net Profit: _____ > _____
Book/Share: _____ > _____
ROE: _____ > _____
ROA: _____ > _____

## analyst ratings

| Strong Buy | | | Mod Buy |
| Hold | | | |
| Strong Sell | | | Mod Sell |
| Insiders | Buy | Sell | |

## sec filings (10K/10Q)

CEO: Name _____ Years _____ Prior _____
CFO: Name _____ Years _____ Prior _____
Rational: _____ Moat Size: _____
New Products or Acquisitions: _____
_____
Competitive Advantage: _____
_____
_____
Profit Engine: _____
_____

## research

Company Web Site: _____
Wikipedia.org: _____
Google News: _____
CNBC.com: _____
Fortune.com: _____
BusinessWeek.com: _____

# Stock Tracker

company ............................................................ symbol ......... date ...............

attention trigger ........................................................................................

........................................................................................

## graph (1 year)

0

-12mo            -6mo          T

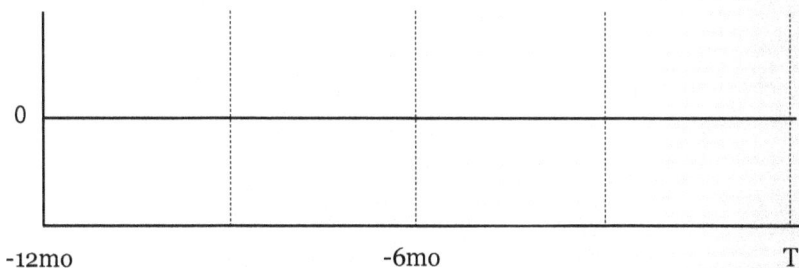

## quote/financial highlights

Stock Price: _____
EPS: _____
P/E: _____
Market Cap: _____
Div (Yield): _____
Debt/Equity: _____
EPS Growth: Pos ____ Neg ____

## quote/financial highlights

EBIT:     Pos ____ Neg ____
Assets:    Pos ____ Neg ____
LT Debt:   Pos ____ Neg ____

## value price

EPS*10: _____
EPS*15: _____
Book/Share: _____

## key ratios

| | Company | Industry |
|---|---|---|
| SG: Sales | _____ | _____ |
| G: Income | _____ | _____ |
| P: Price/Sales | _____ | _____ |
| P: Price/Book | _____ | _____ |
| P: Price/CF | _____ | _____ |
| M: Net | _____ | _____ |
| I: ROE | _____ | _____ |
| I: ROA | _____ | _____ |
| I: ROC | _____ | _____ |

## personal call

| price | bargain | fair | high | crazy | decision | buy | wait | ignore |
|---|---|---|---|---|---|---|---|---|

13

# Stock Tracker

Personal Investment Journal
by bookmark™

company .........................................................................................................................

industry ............................................... industry leader .........................................

## key ratios: 10 yr comparisons

P/E: _____ > _____
P/S: _____ > _____
P/B: _____ > _____
Net Profit: _____ > _____
Book/Share: _____ > _____
ROE: _____ > _____
ROA: _____ > _____

## analyst ratings

| | | |
|---|---|---|
| Strong Buy | | Mod Buy |
| | Hold | |
| Strong Sell | | Mod Sell |
| | Buy | Sell |
| Insiders | | |

## sec filings (10K/10Q)

CEO: Name _____ Years _____ Prior _____
CFO: Name _____ Years _____ Prior _____
Rational: _____ Moat Size: _____
New Products or Acquisitions: _____
_____
Competitive Advantage: _____
_____
_____
Profit Engine: _____
_____

## research

Company Web Site: _____
Wikipedia.org: _____
Google News: _____
CNBC.com: _____
Fortune.com: _____
BusinessWeek.com: _____

# Stock Tracker

company ................................................................ symbol .......... date ..............

attention trigger ........................................................................................

........................................................................................................

## graph (1 year)

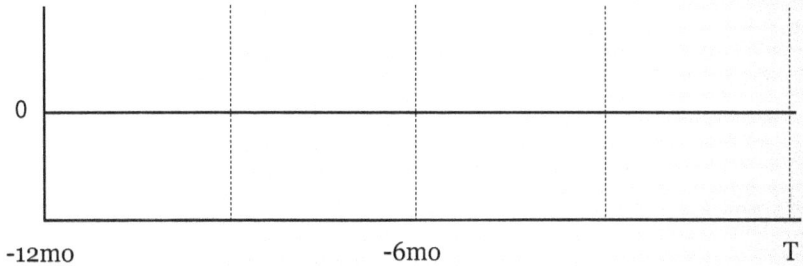

0

-12mo                              -6mo                                    T

## quote/financial highlights

Stock Price: _____
EPS: _____
P/E: _____
Market Cap: _____
Div (Yield): _____
Debt/Equity: _____
EPS Growth: Pos ____ Neg ____

## quote/financial highlights

EBIT:      Pos ____ Neg ____
Assets:    Pos ____ Neg ____
LT Debt:   Pos ____ Neg ____

## value price

EPS*10: _____
EPS*15: _____
Book/Share: _____

## key ratios

| | Company | Industry |
|---|---|---|
| SG: Sales | _____ | _____ |
| G: Income | _____ | _____ |
| P: Price/Sales | _____ | _____ |
| P: Price/Book | _____ | _____ |
| P: Price/CF | _____ | _____ |
| M: Net | _____ | _____ |
| I: ROE | _____ | _____ |
| I: ROA | _____ | _____ |
| I: ROC | _____ | _____ |

## personal call

| price | bargain | fair | high | crazy | decision | buy | wait | ignore |
|---|---|---|---|---|---|---|---|---|

# Stock Tracker

company ................................................................................................................

industry .............................................. industry leader ..........................................

## key ratios: 10 yr comparisons

P/E:            _____ > _____
P/S:            _____ > _____
P/B:            _____ > _____
Net Profit:     _____ > _____
Book/Share:  _____ > _____
ROE:           _____ > _____
ROA:           _____ > _____

## analyst ratings

| Strong Buy | | | Mod Buy |
|---|---|---|---|
| | Hold | | |
| Strong Sell | | | Mod Sell |
| | Buy | Sell | |
| Insiders | | | |

## sec filings (10K/10Q)

CEO: Name _____ Years _____ Prior _____
CFO: Name _____ Years _____ Prior _____
Rational: _____ Moat Size: _____
New Products or Acquisitions: _____
_____

Competitive Advantage: _____
_____
_____

Profit Engine: _____
_____

## research

Company Web Site: _____
Wikipedia.org:       _____
Google News:        _____
CNBC.com:           _____
Fortune.com:        _____
BusinessWeek.com: _____

# Stock Tracker

Personal Investment Journal
by bookmark™

company ........................................................... symbol ......... date ...............

attention trigger ...................................................................................

.......................................................................................................

## graph (1 year)

0 _____

-12mo                    -6mo                    T

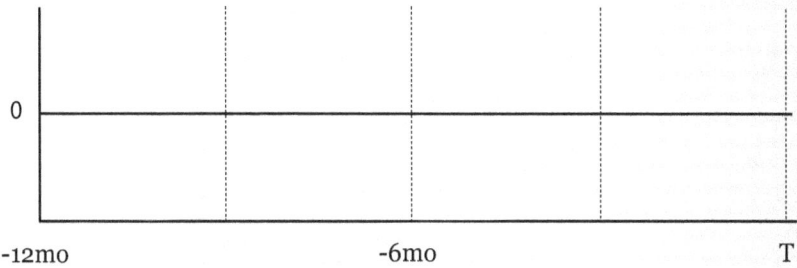

## quote/financial highlights

Stock Price: _____
EPS:         _____
P/E:         _____
Market Cap:  _____
Div (Yield): _____
Debt/Equity: _____
EPS Growth: Pos ___ Neg ___

## value price

EPS*10:     _____
EPS*15:     _____
Book/Share: _____

## quote/financial highlights

EBIT:     Pos ___ Neg ___
Assets:   Pos ___ Neg ___
LT Debt:  Pos ___ Neg ___

## key ratios

| key ratios | Company | Industry |
|---|---|---|
| SG: Sales | ___ | ___ |
| G: Income | ___ | ___ |
| P: Price/Sales | ___ | ___ |
| P: Price/Book | ___ | ___ |
| P: Price/CF | ___ | ___ |
| M: Net | ___ | ___ |
| I: ROE | ___ | ___ |
| I: ROA | ___ | ___ |
| I: ROC | ___ | ___ |

## personal call

| price | bargain | fair | high | crazy | decision | buy | wait | ignore |
|---|---|---|---|---|---|---|---|---|

17

# Stock Tracker

company .............................................................................................................

industry ........................................ industry leader .........................................

## key ratios: 10 yr comparisons

P/E:        _____ > _____
P/S:        _____ > _____
P/B:        _____ > _____
Net Profit:  _____ > _____
Book/Share: _____ > _____
ROE:        _____ > _____
ROA:        _____ > _____

## analyst ratings

| Strong Buy | | Mod Buy |
|---|---|---|
| | Hold | |
| Strong Sell | | Mod Sell |
| | Buy | Sell |
| Insiders | | |

## sec filings (10K/10Q)

CEO: Name _____ Years _____ Prior _____
CFO: Name _____ Years _____ Prior _____
Rational:_____ Moat Size: _____
New Products or Acquisitions:_____
_____
Competitive Advantage:_____
_____
_____
Profit Engine:_____
_____

## research

Company Web Site: _____
Wikipedia.org:    _____
Google News:      _____
CNBC.com:         _____
Fortune.com:      _____
BusinessWeek.com:_____

## Stock Tracker

Personal Investment Journal
by bookmark™

company ................................................. symbol ......... date ...............

attention trigger ...................................................................

.................................................................................................

graph (1 year)

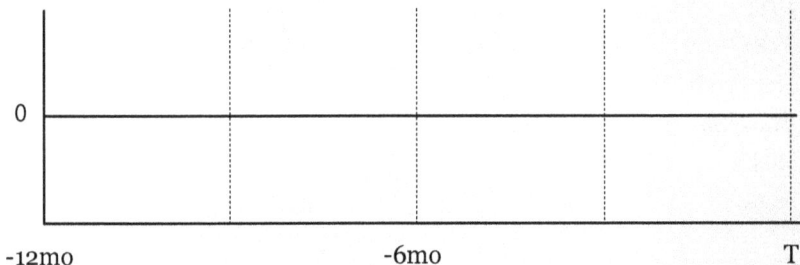

0

-12mo          -6mo                                    T

| quote/financial highlights | value price |
|---|---|
| Stock Price: _____ | EPS*10: _____ |
| EPS: _____ | EPS*15: _____ |
| P/E: _____ | Book/Share: _____ |
| Market Cap: _____ | |
| Div (Yield): _____ | |

**key ratios**    Company   Industry

Debt/Equity: _____

EPS Growth: Pos ____ Neg ____

| key ratios | Company | Industry |
|---|---|---|
| SG: Sales | _____ | _____ |
| G: Income | _____ | _____ |
| P: Price/Sales | _____ | _____ |
| P: Price/Book | _____ | _____ |
| P: Price/CF | _____ | _____ |
| M: Net | _____ | _____ |
| I: ROE | _____ | _____ |
| I: ROA | _____ | _____ |
| I: ROC | _____ | _____ |

### quote/financial highlights

EBIT:  Pos ____ Neg ____

Assets:  Pos ____ Neg ____

LT Debt:  Pos ____ Neg ____

## personal call

| price | bargain | fair | high | crazy | decision | buy | wait | ignore |
|---|---|---|---|---|---|---|---|---|

# Stock Tracker

company ...........................................................................................................

industry ................................................ industry leader ......................................

---

## key ratios: 10 yr comparisons

P/E:  _____ > _____
P/S:  _____ > _____
P/B:  _____ > _____
Net Profit:  _____ > _____
Book/Share:  _____ > _____
ROE:  _____ > _____
ROA:  _____ > _____

## analyst ratings

| | | |
|---|---|---|
| Strong Buy | | Mod Buy |
| | Hold | |
| Strong Sell | | Mod Sell |
| | Buy | Sell |
| Insiders | | |

---

## sec filings (10K/10Q)

CEO: Name _____ Years _____ Prior _____

CFO: Name _____ Years _____ Prior _____

Rational: _____ Moat Size: _____

New Products or Acquisitions: _____
_____

Competitive Advantage: _____
_____
_____

Profit Engine: _____
_____

---

## research

Company Web Site: _____
Wikipedia.org: _____
Google News: _____
CNBC.com: _____
Fortune.com: _____
BusinessWeek.com: _____

# Stock Tracker

company ........................................................ symbol .......... date ...............

attention trigger ...........................................................................

..................................................................................................

## graph (1 year)

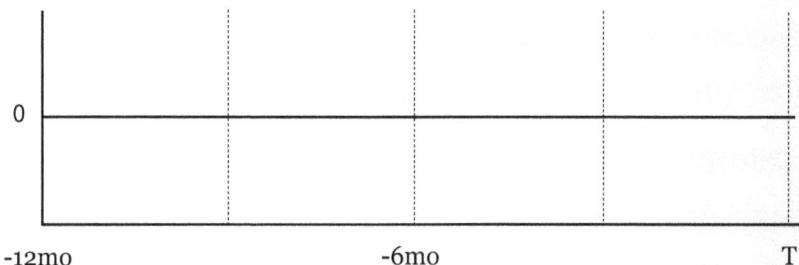

0

-12mo                    -6mo                              T

## quote/financial highlights

Stock Price: _____
EPS:         _____
P/E:         _____
Market Cap:  _____
Div (Yield): _____
Debt/Equity: _____
EPS Growth: Pos _____ Neg _____

## value price

EPS*10:      _____
EPS*15:      _____
Book/Share:  _____

## quote/financial highlights

EBIT:    Pos _____ Neg _____
Assets:  Pos _____ Neg _____
LT Debt: Pos _____ Neg _____

## key ratios

| | Company | Industry |
|---|---|---|
| SG: Sales | _____ | _____ |
| G: Income | _____ | _____ |
| P: Price/Sales | _____ | _____ |
| P: Price/Book | _____ | _____ |
| P: Price/CF | _____ | _____ |
| M: Net | _____ | _____ |
| I: ROE | _____ | _____ |
| I: ROA | _____ | _____ |
| I: ROC | _____ | _____ |

## personal call

| price | bargain | fair | high | crazy | decision | buy | wait | ignore |
|---|---|---|---|---|---|---|---|---|

# Stock Tracker

company .........................................................................................................................

industry ....................................... industry leader .................................................

## key ratios: 10 yr comparisons

P/E:          _____ > _____
P/S:          _____ > _____
P/B:          _____ > _____
Net Profit:   _____ > _____
Book/Share:  _____ > _____
ROE:          _____ > _____
ROA:          _____ > _____

## analyst ratings

| Strong Buy | | Mod Buy |
| Hold | | |
| Strong Sell | | Mod Sell |
| Buy | Sell | |
| Insiders | | |

## sec filings (10K/10Q)

CEO: Name _____ Years _____ Prior _____
CFO: Name _____ Years _____ Prior _____
Rational: _____ Moat Size: _____
New Products or Acquisitions: _____
_____
Competitive Advantage: _____
_____
_____
Profit Engine: _____
_____

## research

Company Web Site: _____
Wikipedia.org:    _____
Google News:      _____
CNBC.com:         _____
Fortune.com:      _____
BusinessWeek.com: _____

# Stock Tracker

company .............................................................. symbol ........... date ...............

attention trigger ...............................................................................

..................................................................................................................

## graph (1 year)

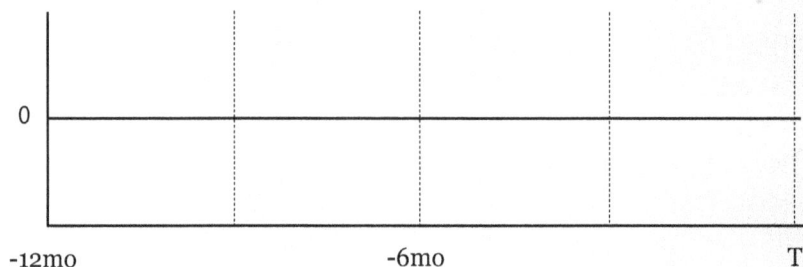

0

-12mo                          -6mo                              T

## quote/financial highlights

Stock Price: _____

EPS: _____

P/E: _____

Market Cap: _____

Div (Yield): _____

Debt/Equity: _____

EPS Growth: Pos ____ Neg ____

## quote/financial highlights

EBIT:        Pos ____ Neg ____

Assets:      Pos ____ Neg ____

LT Debt:     Pos ____ Neg ____

## value price

EPS*10: _____

EPS*15: _____

Book/Share: _____

## key ratios

| | Company | Industry |
|---|---|---|
| SG: Sales | _____ | _____ |
| G: Income | _____ | _____ |
| P: Price/Sales | _____ | _____ |
| P: Price/Book | _____ | _____ |
| P: Price/CF | _____ | _____ |
| M: Net | _____ | _____ |
| I: ROE | _____ | _____ |
| I: ROA | _____ | _____ |
| I: ROC | _____ | _____ |

## personal call

price | bargain | fair | high | crazy   decision | buy | wait | ignore

# Stock Tracker

Personal Investment Journal
by bookmark™

company .........................................................................................................

industry .......................................... industry leader ...........................................

## key ratios: 10 yr comparisons

P/E: _____ > _____
P/S: _____ > _____
P/B: _____ > _____
Net Profit: _____ > _____
Book/Share: _____ > _____
ROE: _____ > _____
ROA: _____ > _____

## analyst ratings

| Strong Buy | | | Mod Buy |
| Hold | | | |
| Strong Sell | | | Mod Sell |
| | Buy | Sell | |
| Insiders | | | |

## sec filings (10K/10Q)

CEO: Name _____ Years _____ Prior _____
CFO: Name _____ Years _____ Prior _____
Rational: _____ Moat Size: _____
New Products or Acquisitions: _____
_____
Competitive Advantage: _____
_____
_____
Profit Engine: _____
_____

## research

Company Web Site: _____
Wikipedia.org: _____
Google News: _____
CNBC.com: _____
Fortune.com: _____
BusinessWeek.com: _____

# Stock Tracker

Personal Investment Journal
by bookmark™

company ................................................................ symbol ......... date ..............

attention trigger ...................................................................................

................................................................................................................

## graph (1 year)

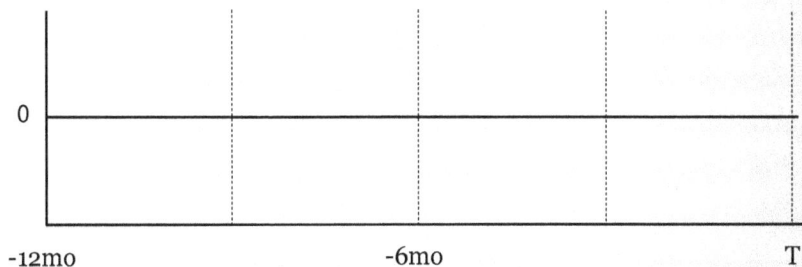

0

-12mo                        -6mo                              T

## quote/financial highlights

Stock Price: _____
EPS: _____
P/E: _____
Market Cap: _____
Div (Yield): _____
Debt/Equity: _____
EPS Growth: Pos ____ Neg ____

## quote/financial highlights

EBIT:      Pos ____ Neg ____
Assets:    Pos ____ Neg ____
LT Debt:   Pos ____ Neg ____

## value price

EPS*10:      _____
EPS*15:      _____
Book/Share: _____

## key ratios

| key ratios | Company | Industry |
|---|---|---|
| SG: Sales | _____ | _____ |
| G: Income | _____ | _____ |
| P: Price/Sales | _____ | _____ |
| P: Price/Book | _____ | _____ |
| P: Price/CF | _____ | _____ |
| M: Net | _____ | _____ |
| I: ROE | _____ | _____ |
| I: ROA | _____ | _____ |
| I: ROC | _____ | _____ |

## personal call

| price | bargain | fair | high | crazy | decision | buy | wait | ignore |

25

# Stock Tracker

company ................................................................................................................

industry ........................................... industry leader .....................................

## key ratios: 10 yr comparisons

P/E: _____ > _____
P/S: _____ > _____
P/B: _____ > _____
Net Profit: _____ > _____
Book/Share: _____ > _____
ROE: _____ > _____
ROA: _____ > _____

## analyst ratings

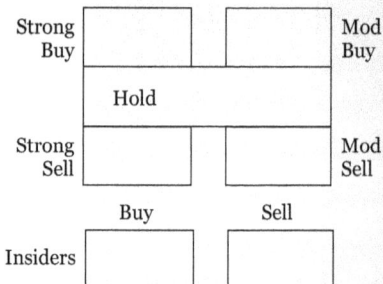

| Strong Buy | | Mod Buy |
|---|---|---|
| | Hold | |
| Strong Sell | | Mod Sell |
| Buy | Sell | |
| Insiders | | |

## sec filings (10K/10Q)

CEO: Name _____ Years _____ Prior _____
CFO: Name _____ Years _____ Prior _____
Rational: _____ Moat Size: _____
New Products or Acquisitions: _____

Competitive Advantage: _____

Profit Engine: _____

## research

Company Web Site: _____
Wikipedia.org: _____
Google News: _____
CNBC.com: _____
Fortune.com: _____
BusinessWeek.com: _____

# Stock Tracker

Personal Investment Journal
by **bookmark**™

company ............................................................. symbol .......... date ..............

attention trigger ........................................................................................

............................................................................................................................

## graph (1 year)

0 ——————————————————————————————————

-12mo                    -6mo                                    T

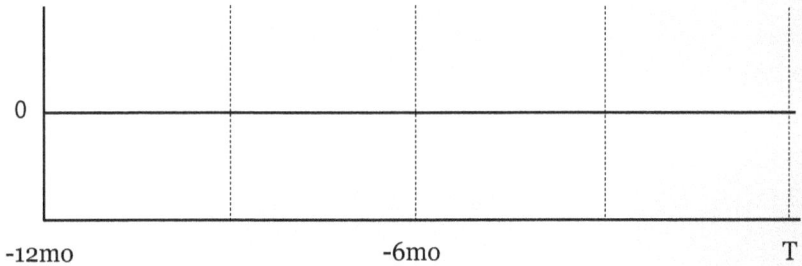

## quote/financial highlights

Stock Price: _____
EPS: _____
P/E: _____
Market Cap: _____
Div (Yield): _____
Debt/Equity: _____
EPS Growth: Pos ____ Neg ____

## quote/financial highlights

EBIT:        Pos ____ Neg ____
Assets:      Pos ____ Neg ____
LT Debt:     Pos ____ Neg ____

## value price

EPS*10: _____
EPS*15: _____
Book/Share: _____

## key ratios

| | Company | Industry |
| --- | --- | --- |
| SG: Sales | _____ | _____ |
| G: Income | _____ | _____ |
| P: Price/Sales | _____ | _____ |
| P: Price/Book | _____ | _____ |
| P: Price/CF | _____ | _____ |
| M: Net | _____ | _____ |
| I: ROE | _____ | _____ |
| I: ROA | _____ | _____ |
| I: ROC | _____ | _____ |

## personal call

| price | bargain | fair | high | crazy | decision | buy | wait | ignore |

27

# Stock Tracker

Personal Investment Journal
by bookmark™

company ................................................................................................

industry ........................................... industry leader ..............................

## key ratios: 10 yr comparisons

P/E: _____ > _____
P/S: _____ > _____
P/B: _____ > _____
Net Profit: _____ > _____
Book/Share: _____ > _____
ROE: _____ > _____
ROA: _____ > _____

## analyst ratings

| Strong Buy | | Mod Buy |
|---|---|---|
| | Hold | |
| Strong Sell | | Mod Sell |
| | Buy | Sell |
| Insiders | | |

## sec filings (10K/10Q)

CEO: Name _____ Years _____ Prior _____
CFO: Name _____ Years _____ Prior _____
Rational: _____ Moat Size: _____
New Products or Acquisitions: _____
_____
Competitive Advantage: _____
_____
_____
Profit Engine: _____
_____

## research

Company Web Site: _____
Wikipedia.org: _____
Google News: _____
CNBC.com: _____
Fortune.com: _____
BusinessWeek.com: _____

# Stock Tracker

company ............................................................ symbol .......... date ...............

attention trigger ..............................................................................

..............................................................................................

## graph (1 year)

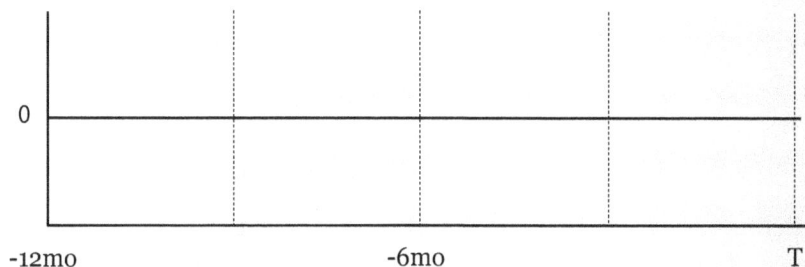

0

-12mo                    -6mo                              T

## quote/financial highlights

Stock Price: _____

EPS: _____

P/E: _____

Market Cap: _____

Div (Yield): _____

Debt/Equity: _____

EPS Growth: Pos ____ Neg ____

## quote/financial highlights

EBIT:      Pos ____ Neg ____

Assets:    Pos ____ Neg ____

LT Debt:   Pos ____ Neg ____

## value price

EPS*10: _____

EPS*15: _____

Book/Share: _____

## key ratios

| | Company | Industry |
|---|---|---|
| SG: Sales | _____ | _____ |
| G: Income | _____ | _____ |
| P: Price/Sales | _____ | _____ |
| P: Price/Book | _____ | _____ |
| P: Price/CF | _____ | _____ |
| M: Net | _____ | _____ |
| I: ROE | _____ | _____ |
| I: ROA | _____ | _____ |
| I: ROC | _____ | _____ |

## personal call

| price | bargain | fair | high | crazy | decision | buy | wait | ignore |
|---|---|---|---|---|---|---|---|---|

# Stock Tracker

company .................................................................................................................

industry ............................................. industry leader ........................................

## key ratios: 10 yr comparisons

P/E: _____ > _____
P/S: _____ > _____
P/B: _____ > _____
Net Profit: _____ > _____
Book/Share: _____ > _____
ROE: _____ > _____
ROA: _____ > _____

## analyst ratings

| | Strong Buy | | | Mod Buy |
|---|---|---|---|---|
| | | Hold | | |
| | Strong Sell | | | Mod Sell |
| | Buy | | Sell | |
| Insiders | | | | |

## sec filings (10K/10Q)

CEO: Name _____ Years _____ Prior _____
CFO: Name _____ Years _____ Prior _____
Rational: _____ Moat Size: _____
New Products or Acquisitions: _____
_____
Competitive Advantage: _____
_____
_____
Profit Engine: _____
_____

## research

Company Web Site: _____
Wikipedia.org: _____
Google News: _____
CNBC.com: _____
Fortune.com: _____
BusinessWeek.com: _____

## Stock Tracker

company ............................................................ symbol ......... date ..............

attention trigger ........................................................................................

.......................................................................................................................

---

### graph (1 year)

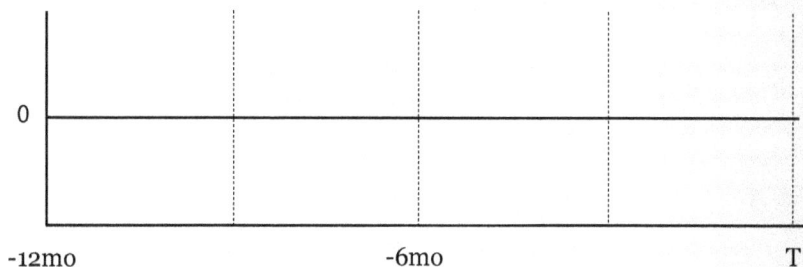

0

-12mo          -6mo                    T

---

### quote/financial highlights

Stock Price: _____
EPS: _____
P/E: _____
Market Cap: _____
Div (Yield): _____
Debt/Equity: _____
EPS Growth: Pos ____ Neg ____

### quote/financial highlights

EBIT:    Pos ____ Neg ____
Assets:  Pos ____ Neg ____
LT Debt: Pos ____ Neg ____

### value price

EPS*10: _____
EPS*15: _____
Book/Share: _____

### key ratios

| | Company | Industry |
|---|---|---|
| SG: Sales | _____ | _____ |
| G: Income | _____ | _____ |
| P: Price/Sales | _____ | _____ |
| P: Price/Book | _____ | _____ |
| P: Price/CF | _____ | _____ |
| M: Net | _____ | _____ |
| I: ROE | _____ | _____ |
| I: ROA | _____ | _____ |
| I: ROC | _____ | _____ |

---

### personal call

| price | bargain | fair | high | crazy | decision | buy | wait | ignore | 31 |
|---|---|---|---|---|---|---|---|---|---|

# Stock Tracker

Personal Investment Journal
by bookmark™

company .........................................................................................................

industry .......................................... industry leader ...........................................

## key ratios: 10 yr comparisons

P/E:            _____ > _____
P/S:            _____ > _____
P/B:            _____ > _____
Net Profit:    _____ > _____
Book/Share: _____ > _____
ROE:            _____ > _____
ROA:            _____ > _____

## analyst ratings

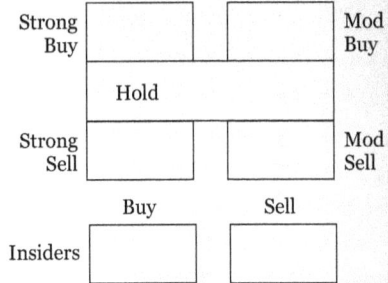

| | | | |
|---|---|---|---|
| Strong Buy | | | Mod Buy |
| | Hold | | |
| Strong Sell | | | Mod Sell |
| | Buy | Sell | |
| Insiders | | | |

## sec filings (10K/10Q)

CEO: Name _____ Years _____ Prior _____
CFO: Name _____ Years _____ Prior _____
Rational: _____ Moat Size: _____
New Products or Acquisitions: _____
_____

Competitive Advantage: _____
_____
_____

Profit Engine: _____
_____

## research

Company Web Site: _____
Wikipedia.org:        _____
Google News:         _____
CNBC.com:             _____
Fortune.com:          _____
BusinessWeek.com: _____

# Stock Tracker

company ........................................................... symbol .......... date ...............

attention trigger ...................................................................................

..................................................................................................................

## graph (1 year)

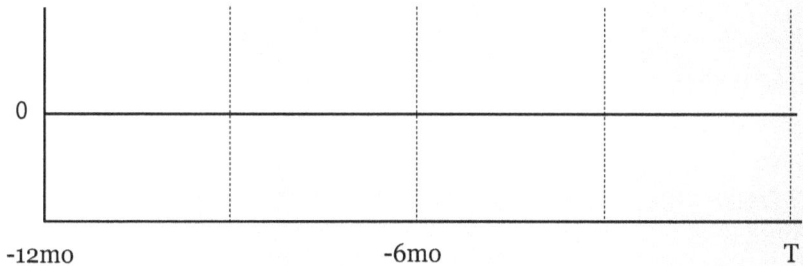

0

-12mo          -6mo          T

## quote/financial highlights

Stock Price: _____

EPS: _____

P/E: _____

Market Cap: _____

Div (Yield): _____

Debt/Equity: _____

EPS Growth: Pos ____ Neg ____

## quote/financial highlights

EBIT:        Pos ____ Neg ____

Assets:      Pos ____ Neg ____

LT Debt:     Pos ____ Neg ____

## value price

EPS*10: _____

EPS*15: _____

Book/Share: _____

## key ratios

| | Company | Industry |
|---|---|---|
| SG: Sales | _____ | _____ |
| G: Income | _____ | _____ |
| P: Price/Sales | _____ | _____ |
| P: Price/Book | _____ | _____ |
| P: Price/CF | _____ | _____ |
| M: Net | _____ | _____ |
| I: ROE | _____ | _____ |
| I: ROA | _____ | _____ |
| I: ROC | _____ | _____ |

## personal call

| price | bargain | fair | high | crazy | decision | buy | wait | ignore |
|---|---|---|---|---|---|---|---|---|

# Stock Tracker

Personal Investment Journal
by bookmark™

company .................................................................................................

industry ........................................... industry leader .............................

## key ratios: 10 yr comparisons

P/E: _____ > _____
P/S: _____ > _____
P/B: _____ > _____
Net Profit: _____ > _____
Book/Share: _____ > _____
ROE: _____ > _____
ROA: _____ > _____

## analyst ratings

| Strong Buy | | | Mod Buy |
| Hold | | | |
| Strong Sell | | | Mod Sell |
| | Buy | Sell | |
| Insiders | | | |

## sec filings (10K/10Q)

CEO: Name _____ Years _____ Prior _____
CFO: Name _____ Years _____ Prior _____
Rational: _____ Moat Size: _____
New Products or Acquisitions: _____
_____
Competitive Advantage: _____
_____
_____
Profit Engine: _____
_____

## research

Company Web Site: _____
Wikipedia.org: _____
Google News: _____
CNBC.com: _____
Fortune.com: _____
BusinessWeek.com: _____

# Stock Tracker

company .................................................... symbol .......... date ...............

attention trigger ...................................................................................

..............................................................................................................

## graph (1 year)

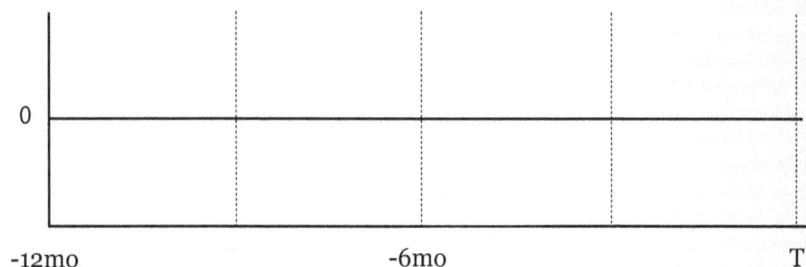

0

-12mo                    -6mo                              T

## quote/financial highlights

Stock Price: _____

EPS: _____

P/E: _____

Market Cap: _____

Div (Yield): _____

Debt/Equity: _____

EPS Growth: Pos ____ Neg ____

## quote/financial highlights

EBIT:        Pos ____ Neg ____

Assets:      Pos ____ Neg ____

LT Debt:     Pos ____ Neg ____

## value price

EPS*10: _____

EPS*15: _____

Book/Share: _____

## key ratios

| | Company | Industry |
|---|---|---|
| SG: Sales | _____ | _____ |
| G: Income | _____ | _____ |
| P: Price/Sales | _____ | _____ |
| P: Price/Book | _____ | _____ |
| P: Price/CF | _____ | _____ |
| M: Net | _____ | _____ |
| I: ROE | _____ | _____ |
| I: ROA | _____ | _____ |
| I: ROC | _____ | _____ |

## personal call

| price | bargain | fair | high | crazy | decision | buy | wait | ignore |
|---|---|---|---|---|---|---|---|---|

35

# Stock Tracker

company ........................................................................................................

industry ........................................... industry leader ...........................................

## key ratios: 10 yr comparisons

P/E: _____ > _____
P/S: _____ > _____
P/B: _____ > _____
Net Profit: _____ > _____
Book/Share: _____ > _____
ROE: _____ > _____
ROA: _____ > _____

## analyst ratings

| Strong Buy | | Mod Buy |
|---|---|---|
| | Hold | |
| Strong Sell | | Mod Sell |
| | Buy | Sell |
| Insiders | | |

## sec filings (10K/10Q)

CEO: Name _____ Years _____ Prior _____

CFO: Name _____ Years _____ Prior _____

Rational:_____ Moat Size: _____

New Products or Acquisitions:_____

_____

Competitive Advantage:_____

_____

_____

Profit Engine:_____

_____

## research

Company Web Site: _____

Wikipedia.org: _____

Google News: _____

CNBC.com: _____

Fortune.com: _____

BusinessWeek.com:_____

# Stock Tracker

company ........................................................... symbol ......... date ...............

attention trigger ........................................................................................

..........................................................................................................

## graph (1 year)

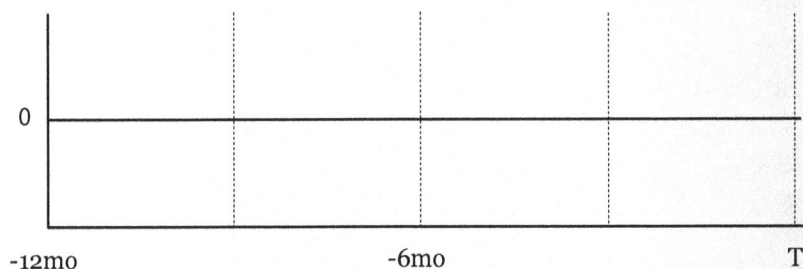

0

-12mo                          -6mo                              T

## quote/financial highlights

Stock Price: _____
EPS: _____
P/E: _____
Market Cap: _____
Div (Yield): _____
Debt/Equity: _____
EPS Growth: Pos ____ Neg ____

## quote/financial highlights

EBIT:        Pos ____ Neg ____
Assets:      Pos ____ Neg ____
LT Debt:     Pos ____ Neg ____

## value price

EPS*10: _____
EPS*15: _____
Book/Share: _____

| key ratios | Company | Industry |
|---|---|---|
| SG: Sales | _____ | _____ |
| G: Income | _____ | _____ |
| P: Price/Sales | _____ | _____ |
| P: Price/Book | _____ | _____ |
| P: Price/CF | _____ | _____ |
| M: Net | _____ | _____ |
| I: ROE | _____ | _____ |
| I: ROA | _____ | _____ |
| I: ROC | _____ | _____ |

## personal call

| price | bargain | fair | high | crazy | decision | buy | wait | ignore |
|---|---|---|---|---|---|---|---|---|

# Stock Tracker

company ..................................................................................................................

industry ............................................... industry leader ...................................

---

## key ratios: 10 yr comparisons

P/E: _____ > _____
P/S: _____ > _____
P/B: _____ > _____
Net Profit: _____ > _____
Book/Share: _____ > _____
ROE: _____ > _____
ROA: _____ > _____

## analyst ratings

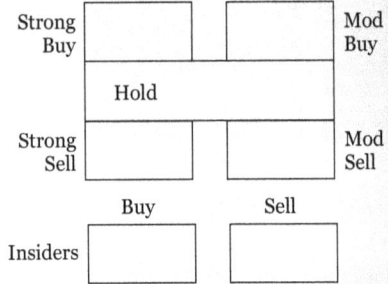

| | | | |
|---|---|---|---|
| Strong Buy | | | Mod Buy |
| | Hold | | |
| Strong Sell | | | Mod Sell |
| | Buy | Sell | |
| Insiders | | | |

---

## sec filings (10K/10Q)

CEO: Name _____ Years _____ Prior _____

CFO: Name _____ Years _____ Prior _____

Rational: _____ Moat Size: _____

New Products or Acquisitions: _____

_____

Competitive Advantage: _____

_____

_____

Profit Engine: _____

_____

---

## research

Company Web Site: _____

Wikipedia.org: _____

Google News: _____

CNBC.com: _____

Fortune.com: _____

BusinessWeek.com: _____

# Stock Tracker

company ........................................................ symbol ......... date ............

attention trigger ....................................................................

................................................................................

## graph (1 year)

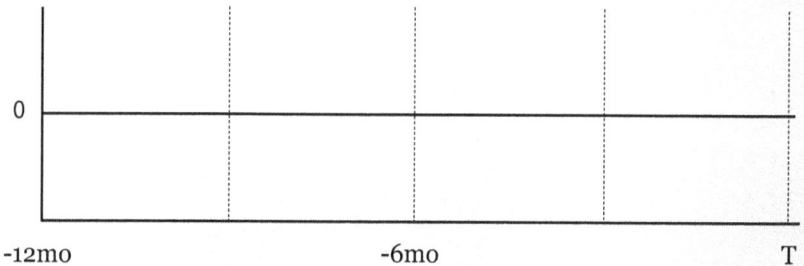

0

-12mo                    -6mo                    T

## quote/financial highlights

Stock Price: _____

EPS: _____

P/E: _____

Market Cap: _____

Div (Yield): _____

Debt/Equity: _____

EPS Growth: Pos ____ Neg ____

## quote/financial highlights

EBIT:    Pos ____ Neg ____

Assets:  Pos ____ Neg ____

LT Debt: Pos ____ Neg ____

## value price

EPS*10: _____

EPS*15: _____

Book/Share: _____

## key ratios

| | Company | Industry |
|---|---|---|
| SG: Sales | _____ | _____ |
| G: Income | _____ | _____ |
| P: Price/Sales | _____ | _____ |
| P: Price/Book | _____ | _____ |
| P: Price/CF | _____ | _____ |
| M: Net | _____ | _____ |
| I: ROE | _____ | _____ |
| I: ROA | _____ | _____ |
| I: ROC | _____ | _____ |

## personal call

| price | bargain | fair | high | crazy | decision | buy | wait | ignore |

# Stock Tracker

company .......................................................................................................................

industry ............................................ industry leader .........................................

## key ratios: 10 yr comparisons

P/E: _____ > _____
P/S: _____ > _____
P/B: _____ > _____
Net Profit: _____ > _____
Book/Share: _____ > _____
ROE: _____ > _____
ROA: _____ > _____

## analyst ratings

| Strong Buy | | Mod Buy |
|---|---|---|
| | Hold | |
| Strong Sell | | Mod Sell |
| Buy | Sell | |
| Insiders | | |

## sec filings (10K/10Q)

CEO: Name _____ Years _____ Prior _____
CFO: Name _____ Years _____ Prior _____
Rational: _____ Moat Size: _____
New Products or Acquisitions: _____
_____

Competitive Advantage: _____
_____
_____

Profit Engine: _____
_____

## research

Company Web Site: _____
Wikipedia.org: _____
Google News: _____
CNBC.com: _____
Fortune.com: _____
BusinessWeek.com: _____

# Stock Tracker

company ........................................................ symbol .......... date ...............

attention trigger ........................................................................

........................................................................

## graph (1 year)

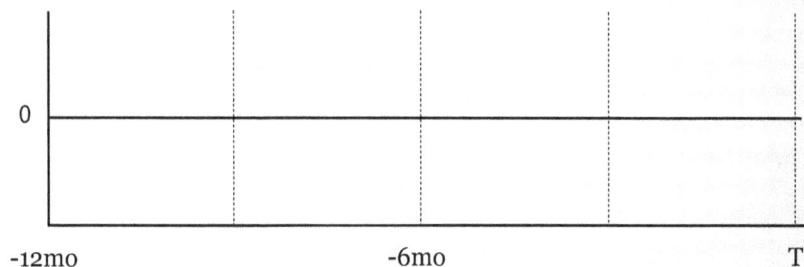

0

-12mo ............................ -6mo ............................ T

## quote/financial highlights

Stock Price: _____

EPS: _____

P/E: _____

Market Cap: _____

Div (Yield): _____

Debt/Equity: _____

EPS Growth: Pos ____ Neg ____

## quote/financial highlights

EBIT:        Pos ____ Neg ____

Assets:      Pos ____ Neg ____

LT Debt:     Pos ____ Neg ____

## value price

EPS*10:      _____

EPS*15:      _____

Book/Share:  _____

## key ratios

| | Company | Industry |
|---|---|---|
| SG: Sales | _____ | _____ |
| G: Income | _____ | _____ |
| P: Price/Sales | _____ | _____ |
| P: Price/Book | _____ | _____ |
| P: Price/CF | _____ | _____ |
| M: Net | _____ | _____ |
| I: ROE | _____ | _____ |
| I: ROA | _____ | _____ |
| I: ROC | _____ | _____ |

## personal call

| price | bargain | fair | high | crazy | decision | buy | wait | ignore |
|---|---|---|---|---|---|---|---|---|

# Stock Tracker

company .........................................................................................................

industry ........................................ industry leader ..................................

## key ratios: 10 yr comparisons

P/E:           _____ > _____
P/S:           _____ > _____
P/B:           _____ > _____
Net Profit:    _____ > _____
Book/Share: _____ > _____
ROE:           _____ > _____
ROA:           _____ > _____

## analyst ratings

| | | |
|---|---|---|
| Strong Buy | | Mod Buy |
| | Hold | |
| Strong Sell | | Mod Sell |

Buy    Sell

Insiders

## sec filings (10K/10Q)

CEO: Name _____ Years _____ Prior _____
CFO: Name _____ Years _____ Prior _____
Rational: _____ Moat Size: _____
New Products or Acquisitions: _____
_____
Competitive Advantage: _____
_____
_____
Profit Engine: _____
_____

## research

Company Web Site: _____
Wikipedia.org: _____
Google News: _____
CNBC.com: _____
Fortune.com: _____
BusinessWeek.com: _____

# Stock Tracker

company ............................................................ symbol ......... date ................

attention trigger .........................................................................................

..........................................................................................................................

## graph (1 year)

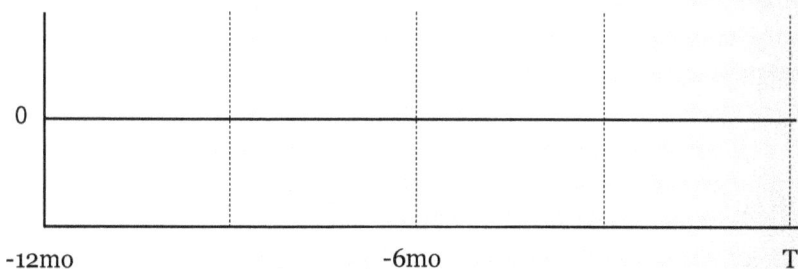

0

-12mo                    -6mo                                    T

## quote/financial highlights

Stock Price: _____
EPS: _____
P/E: _____
Market Cap: _____
Div (Yield): _____
Debt/Equity: _____
EPS Growth: Pos _____ Neg _____

## quote/financial highlights

EBIT:      Pos _____ Neg _____
Assets:    Pos _____ Neg _____
LT Debt:   Pos _____ Neg _____

## value price

EPS*10: _____
EPS*15: _____
Book/Share: _____

## key ratios

| | Company | Industry |
| --- | --- | --- |
| SG: Sales | _____ | _____ |
| G: Income | _____ | _____ |
| P: Price/Sales | _____ | _____ |
| P: Price/Book | _____ | _____ |
| P: Price/CF | _____ | _____ |
| M: Net | _____ | _____ |
| I: ROE | _____ | _____ |
| I: ROA | _____ | _____ |
| I: ROC | _____ | _____ |

## personal call

| price | bargain | fair | high | crazy | decision | buy | wait | ignore |
| --- | --- | --- | --- | --- | --- | --- | --- | --- |

# Stock Tracker

company .................................................................................................................

industry ........................................... industry leader ...........................................

## key ratios: 10 yr comparisons

P/E: _____ > _____
P/S: _____ > _____
P/B: _____ > _____
Net Profit: _____ > _____
Book/Share: _____ > _____
ROE: _____ > _____
ROA: _____ > _____

## analyst ratings

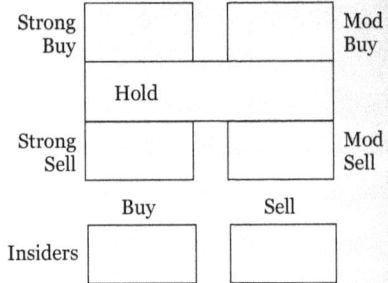

| | Strong Buy | Hold | Mod Buy |
| Strong Sell | | | Mod Sell |
| Insiders | Buy | Sell | |

## sec filings (10K/10Q)

CEO: Name _____ Years _____ Prior _____
CFO: Name _____ Years _____ Prior _____
Rational: _____ Moat Size: _____
New Products or Acquisitions: _____
_____
Competitive Advantage: _____
_____
_____
Profit Engine: _____
_____

## research

Company Web Site: _____
Wikipedia.org: _____
Google News: _____
CNBC.com: _____
Fortune.com: _____
BusinessWeek.com: _____

# Stock Tracker

company ............................................................... symbol .......... date ...............

attention trigger ...........................................................................................

......................................................................................................................

## graph (1 year)

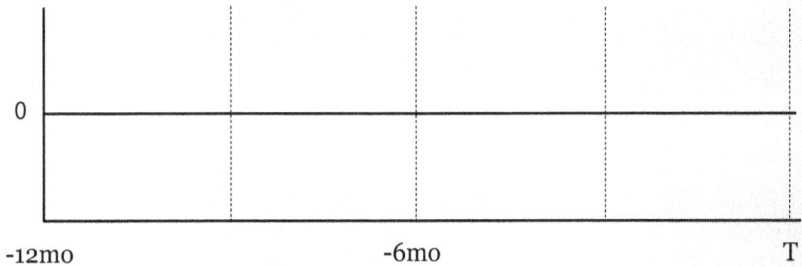

0

-12mo                    -6mo                    T

## quote/financial highlights

Stock Price: _____
EPS: _____
P/E: _____
Market Cap: _____
Div (Yield): _____
Debt/Equity: _____
EPS Growth: Pos ____ Neg ____

## quote/financial highlights

EBIT:      Pos ____ Neg ____
Assets:    Pos ____ Neg ____
LT Debt:   Pos ____ Neg ____

## value price

EPS*10: _____
EPS*15: _____
Book/Share: _____

## key ratios

| | Company | Industry |
|---|---|---|
| SG: Sales | _____ | _____ |
| G: Income | _____ | _____ |
| P: Price/Sales | _____ | _____ |
| P: Price/Book | _____ | _____ |
| P: Price/CF | _____ | _____ |
| M: Net | _____ | _____ |
| I: ROE | _____ | _____ |
| I: ROA | _____ | _____ |
| I: ROC | _____ | _____ |

## personal call

| price | bargain | fair | high | crazy | decision | buy | wait | ignore |
|---|---|---|---|---|---|---|---|---|

45

# Stock Tracker

company ...........................................................................................................

industry ............................................ industry leader ..............................................

## key ratios: 10 yr comparisons

P/E:        _____ > _____
P/S:        _____ > _____
P/B:        _____ > _____
Net Profit: _____ > _____
Book/Share: _____ > _____
ROE:        _____ > _____
ROA:        _____ > _____

## analyst ratings

Strong Buy | [ ] | [ ] | Mod Buy

[ ] Hold

Strong Sell | [ ] | [ ] | Mod Sell

Buy | Sell

Insiders | [ ] | [ ]

## sec filings (10K/10Q)

CEO: Name _____ Years _____ Prior _____
CFO: Name _____ Years _____ Prior _____
Rational: _____ Moat Size: _____
New Products or Acquisitions: _____
_____
Competitive Advantage: _____
_____
_____
Profit Engine: _____
_____

## research

Company Web Site: _____
Wikipedia.org:   _____
Google News:     _____
CNBC.com:        _____
Fortune.com:     _____
BusinessWeek.com: _____

# Stock Tracker

Personal Investment Journal
by bookmark™

company ............................................................ symbol .......... date ................

attention trigger ............................................................................................

............................................................................................................................

## graph (1 year)

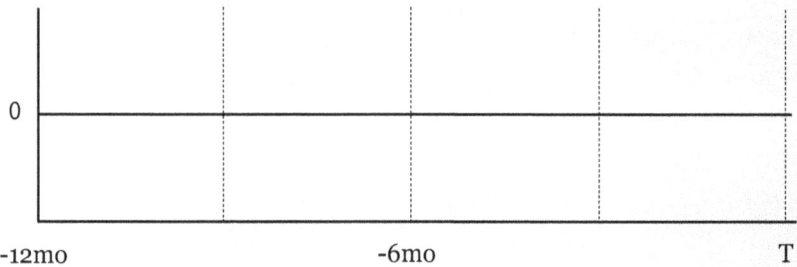

0

-12mo                    -6mo                                   T

## quote/financial highlights

Stock Price: _____

EPS: _____

P/E: _____

Market Cap: _____

Div (Yield): _____

Debt/Equity: _____

EPS Growth: Pos \_\_\_\_ Neg \_\_\_\_

## quote/financial highlights

EBIT: Pos \_\_\_\_ Neg \_\_\_\_

Assets: Pos \_\_\_\_ Neg \_\_\_\_

LT Debt: Pos \_\_\_\_ Neg \_\_\_\_

## value price

EPS*10: _____

EPS*15: _____

Book/Share: _____

## key ratios

| | Company | Industry |
|---|---|---|
| SG: Sales | _____ | _____ |
| G: Income | _____ | _____ |
| P: Price/Sales | _____ | _____ |
| P: Price/Book | _____ | _____ |
| P: Price/CF | _____ | _____ |
| M: Net | _____ | _____ |
| I: ROE | _____ | _____ |
| I: ROA | _____ | _____ |
| I: ROC | _____ | _____ |

## personal call

| price | bargain | fair | high | crazy | decision | buy | wait | ignore |
|---|---|---|---|---|---|---|---|---|

47

# Stock Tracker

Personal Investment Journal
by pro bookmark™

company .........................................................................................................................

industry ........................................ industry leader ........................................

## key ratios: 10 yr comparisons

P/E:          _____ > _____
P/S:          _____ > _____
P/B:          _____ > _____
Net Profit:   _____ > _____
Book/Share:  _____ > _____
ROE:          _____ > _____
ROA:          _____ > _____

## analyst ratings

| Strong Buy | | | Mod Buy |
|---|---|---|---|
| | Hold | | |
| Strong Sell | | | Mod Sell |
| | Buy | Sell | |
| Insiders | | | |

## sec filings (10K/10Q)

CEO: Name _____ Years _____ Prior _____

CFO: Name _____ Years _____ Prior _____

Rational: _____ Moat Size: _____

New Products or Acquisitions: _____

_____

Competitive Advantage: _____

_____

_____

Profit Engine: _____

_____

## research

Company Web Site: _____

Wikipedia.org:      _____

Google News:        _____

CNBC.com:           _____

Fortune.com:        _____

BusinessWeek.com: _____

# Stock Tracker

company ........................................................ symbol .......... date ................

attention trigger ...............................................................................

...............................................................................................

## graph (1 year)

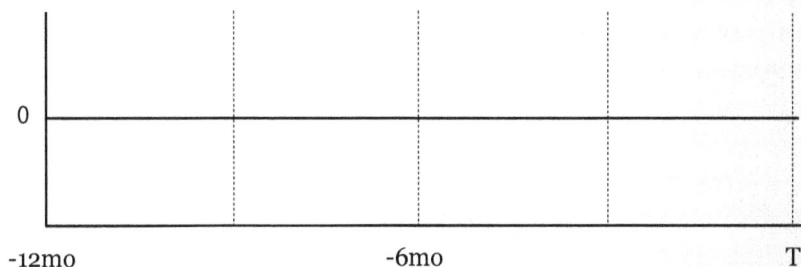

0

-12mo                          -6mo                        T

## quote/financial highlights

Stock Price: _____
EPS: _____
P/E: _____
Market Cap: _____
Div (Yield): _____
Debt/Equity: _____
EPS Growth: Pos ____ Neg ____

## quote/financial highlights

EBIT: Pos ____ Neg ____
Assets: Pos ____ Neg ____
LT Debt: Pos ____ Neg ____

## value price

EPS*10: _____
EPS*15: _____
Book/Share: _____

## key ratios

| | Company | Industry |
| --- | --- | --- |
| SG: Sales | _____ | _____ |
| G: Income | _____ | _____ |
| P: Price/Sales | _____ | _____ |
| P: Price/Book | _____ | _____ |
| P: Price/CF | _____ | _____ |
| M: Net | _____ | _____ |
| I: ROE | _____ | _____ |
| I: ROA | _____ | _____ |
| I: ROC | _____ | _____ |

## personal call

| price | bargain | fair | high | crazy | decision | buy | wait | ignore |
| --- | --- | --- | --- | --- | --- | --- | --- | --- |

# Stock Tracker

Personal Investment Journal
by bookmark™

company .............................................................................................................

industry ..................................... industry leader .....................................

## key ratios: 10 yr comparisons

P/E: _____ > _____
P/S: _____ > _____
P/B: _____ > _____
Net Profit: _____ > _____
Book/Share: _____ > _____
ROE: _____ > _____
ROA: _____ > _____

## analyst ratings

| Strong Buy | | | Mod Buy |
|---|---|---|---|
| | Hold | | |
| Strong Sell | | | Mod Sell |
| | Buy | Sell | |
| Insiders | | | |

## sec filings (10K/10Q)

CEO: Name _____ Years _____ Prior _____

CFO: Name _____ Years _____ Prior _____

Rational: _____ Moat Size: _____

New Products or Acquisitions: _____

Competitive Advantage: _____

Profit Engine: _____

## research

Company Web Site: _____

Wikipedia.org: _____

Google News: _____

CNBC.com: _____

Fortune.com: _____

BusinessWeek.com: _____

# Stock Tracker

company ........................................................... symbol .......... date ..............

attention trigger ...............................................................................

........................................................................................................

## graph (1 year)

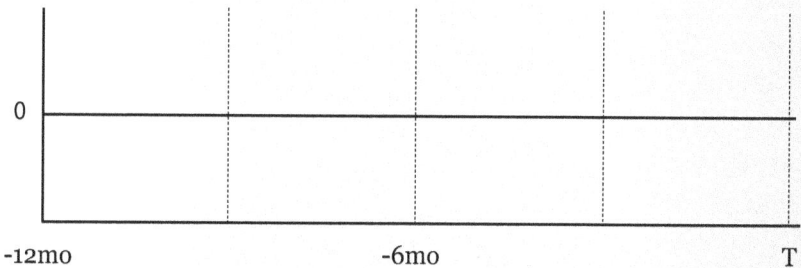

0

-12mo           -6mo           T

## quote/financial highlights

Stock Price: _____

EPS: _____

P/E: _____

Market Cap: _____

Div (Yield): _____

Debt/Equity: _____

EPS Growth: Pos ____ Neg ____

## quote/financial highlights

EBIT: Pos ____ Neg ____

Assets: Pos ____ Neg ____

LT Debt: Pos ____ Neg ____

## value price

EPS*10: _____

EPS*15: _____

Book/Share: _____

## key ratios

| | Company | Industry |
|---|---|---|
| SG: Sales | _____ | _____ |
| G: Income | _____ | _____ |
| P: Price/Sales | _____ | _____ |
| P: Price/Book | _____ | _____ |
| P: Price/CF | _____ | _____ |
| M: Net | _____ | _____ |
| I: ROE | _____ | _____ |
| I: ROA | _____ | _____ |
| I: ROC | _____ | _____ |

## personal call

price | bargain | fair | high | crazy     decision | buy | wait | ignore

# Stock Tracker

Personal Investment Journal
by bookmark™

company ...................................................................................................................

industry ............................................. industry leader ...................................................

## key ratios: 10 yr comparisons

P/E:            _____ > _____
P/S:            _____ > _____
P/B:            _____ > _____
Net Profit:     _____ > _____
Book/Share:     _____ > _____
ROE:            _____ > _____
ROA:            _____ > _____

## analyst ratings

| | Strong Buy | | Mod Buy | |
|---|---|---|---|---|
| | | Hold | | |
| | Strong Sell | | Mod Sell | |
| | Buy | | Sell | |
| | Insiders | | | |

## sec filings (10K/10Q)

CEO: Name _____ Years _____ Prior _____
CFO: Name _____ Years _____ Prior _____
Rational: _____ Moat Size: _____
New Products or Acquisitions: _____
_____
Competitive Advantage: _____
_____
_____
Profit Engine: _____
_____

## research

Company Web Site: _____
Wikipedia.org: _____
Google News: _____
CNBC.com: _____
Fortune.com: _____
BusinessWeek.com: _____

# Stocks of Interest

Personal Investment Journal
by **bookmark**™

1 ...........................................................................................................................................
...........................................................................................................................................
2 ...........................................................................................................................................
...........................................................................................................................................
3 ...........................................................................................................................................
...........................................................................................................................................
4 ...........................................................................................................................................
...........................................................................................................................................
5 ...........................................................................................................................................
...........................................................................................................................................
6 ...........................................................................................................................................
...........................................................................................................................................
7 ...........................................................................................................................................
...........................................................................................................................................
8 ...........................................................................................................................................
...........................................................................................................................................
9 ...........................................................................................................................................
...........................................................................................................................................
10 ...........................................................................................................................................
...........................................................................................................................................
11 ...........................................................................................................................................
...........................................................................................................................................
12 ...........................................................................................................................................
...........................................................................................................................................

# Stocks of Interest

Personal Investment Journal
by bookmark™

13.............................................................................................................
.............................................................................................................
14.............................................................................................................
.............................................................................................................
15.............................................................................................................
.............................................................................................................
16.............................................................................................................
.............................................................................................................
17.............................................................................................................
.............................................................................................................
18.............................................................................................................
.............................................................................................................
19.............................................................................................................
.............................................................................................................
20.............................................................................................................
.............................................................................................................
21.............................................................................................................
.............................................................................................................
22.............................................................................................................
.............................................................................................................
23.............................................................................................................
.............................................................................................................
24.............................................................................................................
.............................................................................................................

# Stock Tracker

company ..................................................... symbol ......... date ...............

attention trigger ....................................................................................

..............................................................................................................

## graph (1 year)

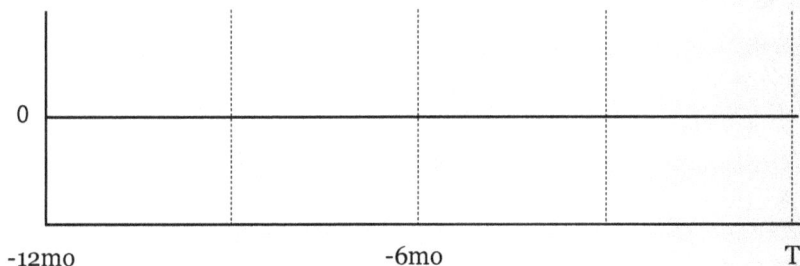

0 ————————————————————————————————————

-12mo                          -6mo                                T

## quote/financial highlights

Stock Price: _____
EPS: _____
P/E: _____
Market Cap: _____
Div (Yield): _____
Debt/Equity: _____
EPS Growth: Pos ____ Neg ____

## quote/financial highlights

EBIT:      Pos ____ Neg ____
Assets:    Pos ____ Neg ____
LT Debt:   Pos ____ Neg ____

## value price

EPS*10: _____
EPS*15: _____
Book/Share: _____

## key ratios       Company   Industry

| | Company | Industry |
|---|---|---|
| SG: Sales | _____ | _____ |
| G: Income | _____ | _____ |
| P: Price/Sales | _____ | _____ |
| P: Price/Book | _____ | _____ |
| P: Price/CF | _____ | _____ |
| M: Net | _____ | _____ |
| I: ROE | _____ | _____ |
| I: ROA | _____ | _____ |
| I: ROC | _____ | _____ |

## personal call

| price | bargain | fair | high | crazy | decision | buy | wait | ignore |
|---|---|---|---|---|---|---|---|---|

# Stock Tracker

company .......................................................................................................................

industry ................................................. industry leader ...................................

## key ratios: 10 yr comparisons

P/E: _____ > _____
P/S: _____ > _____
P/B: _____ > _____
Net Profit: _____ > _____
Book/Share: _____ > _____
ROE: _____ > _____
ROA: _____ > _____

## analyst ratings

| | Strong Buy | | Mod Buy |
|---|---|---|---|
| | | Hold | |
| | Strong Sell | | Mod Sell |
| | Buy | Sell | |
| Insiders | | | |

## sec filings (10K/10Q)

CEO: Name _____ Years _____ Prior _____
CFO: Name _____ Years _____ Prior _____
Rational: _____ Moat Size: _____
New Products or Acquisitions: _____
_____
Competitive Advantage: _____
_____
_____
Profit Engine: _____
_____

## research

Company Web Site: _____
Wikipedia.org: _____
Google News: _____
CNBC.com: _____
Fortune.com: _____
BusinessWeek.com: _____

# Stock Tracker

company ............................................................. symbol .......... date ................

attention trigger ...........................................................................................

.................................................................................................................

## graph (1 year)

```
     |
     |      |            |            |
   0 |_____|_____|_____|_____
     |      |            |            |
     |
   -12mo                -6mo                      T
```

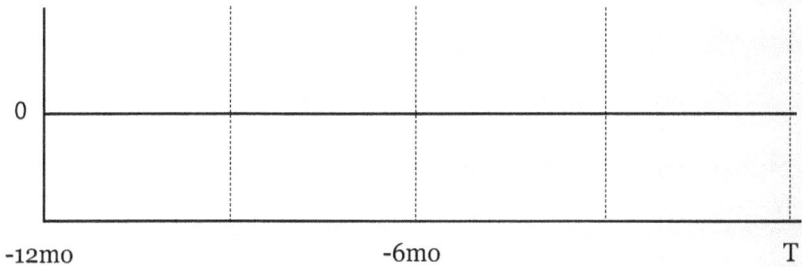

## quote/financial highlights

Stock Price: _____

EPS: _____

P/E: _____

Market Cap: _____

Div (Yield): _____

Debt/Equity: _____

EPS Growth: Pos ____ Neg ____

## quote/financial highlights

EBIT:      Pos ____ Neg ____

Assets:    Pos ____ Neg ____

LT Debt:   Pos ____ Neg ____

## value price

EPS*10: _____

EPS*15: _____

Book/Share: _____

## key ratios

| | Company | Industry |
|---|---|---|
| SG: Sales | _____ | _____ |
| G: Income | _____ | _____ |
| P: Price/Sales | _____ | _____ |
| P: Price/Book | _____ | _____ |
| P: Price/CF | _____ | _____ |
| M: Net | _____ | _____ |
| I: ROE | _____ | _____ |
| I: ROA | _____ | _____ |
| I: ROC | _____ | _____ |

## personal call

| price | bargain | fair | high | crazy | decision | buy | wait | ignore |

# Stock Tracker

company .......................................................................................................................

industry ........................................... industry leader ...........................................

## key ratios: 10 yr comparisons

P/E:          _____ > _____
P/S:          _____ > _____
P/B:          _____ > _____
Net Profit:   _____ > _____
Book/Share:  _____ > _____
ROE:          _____ > _____
ROA:          _____ > _____

## analyst ratings

| Strong Buy | | Mod Buy |
|---|---|---|
| Hold | | |
| Strong Sell | | Mod Sell |
| Buy | Sell | |
| Insiders | | |

## sec filings (10K/10Q)

CEO: Name _____ Years _____ Prior_____

CFO: Name _____ Years _____ Prior_____

Rational:_____ Moat Size: _____

New Products or Acquisitions:_____

_____

Competitive Advantage:_____

_____

_____

Profit Engine:_____

_____

## research

Company Web Site: _____

Wikipedia.org:      _____

Google News:        _____

CNBC.com:           _____

Fortune.com:        _____

BusinessWeek.com: _____

## Stock Tracker

Personal Investment Journal
by bookmark™

company ................................................................... symbol .......... date ...............

attention trigger .........................................................................................

.....................................................................................................................

### graph (1 year)

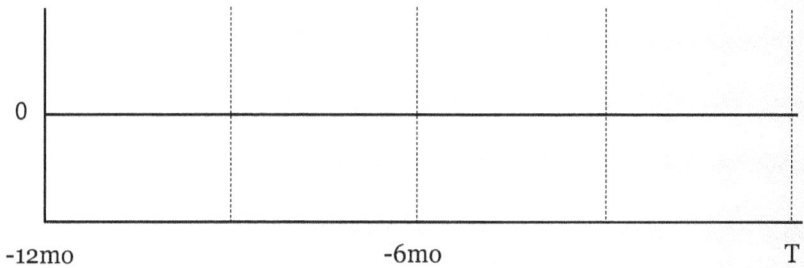

0

-12mo                          -6mo                                   T

### quote/financial highlights

Stock Price: _____
EPS: _____
P/E: _____
Market Cap: _____
Div (Yield): _____
Debt/Equity: _____
EPS Growth: Pos ____ Neg ____

### quote/financial highlights

EBIT:        Pos ____ Neg ____
Assets:      Pos ____ Neg ____
LT Debt:     Pos ____ Neg ____

### value price

EPS*10:      _____
EPS*15:      _____
Book/Share: _____

### key ratios

| | Company | Industry |
|---|---|---|
| SG: Sales | _____ | _____ |
| G: Income | _____ | _____ |
| P: Price/Sales | _____ | _____ |
| P: Price/Book | _____ | _____ |
| P: Price/CF | _____ | _____ |
| M: Net | _____ | _____ |
| I: ROE | _____ | _____ |
| I: ROA | _____ | _____ |
| I: ROC | _____ | _____ |

### personal call

| price | bargain | fair | high | crazy | decision | buy | wait | ignore |
|---|---|---|---|---|---|---|---|---|

# Stock Tracker

company ...................................................................................................................

industry .......................................... industry leader .........................................

## key ratios: 10 yr comparisons

P/E: \_\_\_\_\_ > \_\_\_\_\_
P/S: \_\_\_\_\_ > \_\_\_\_\_
P/B: \_\_\_\_\_ > \_\_\_\_\_
Net Profit: \_\_\_\_\_ > \_\_\_\_\_
Book/Share: \_\_\_\_\_ > \_\_\_\_\_
ROE: \_\_\_\_\_ > \_\_\_\_\_
ROA: \_\_\_\_\_ > \_\_\_\_\_

## analyst ratings

| Strong Buy | | | Mod Buy |
|---|---|---|---|
| | Hold | | |
| Strong Sell | | | Mod Sell |
| | Buy | Sell | |
| Insiders | | | |

## sec filings (10K/10Q)

CEO: Name _____ Years _____ Prior _____
CFO: Name _____ Years _____ Prior _____
Rational: _____ Moat Size: _____
New Products or Acquisitions: _____

Competitive Advantage: _____

Profit Engine: _____

## research

Company Web Site: _____
Wikipedia.org: _____
Google News: _____
CNBC.com: _____
Fortune.com: _____

BusinessWeek.com: _____

# Stock Tracker

company .................................................... symbol ......... date ...............

attention trigger ................................................................................

................................................................................................................

## graph (1 year)

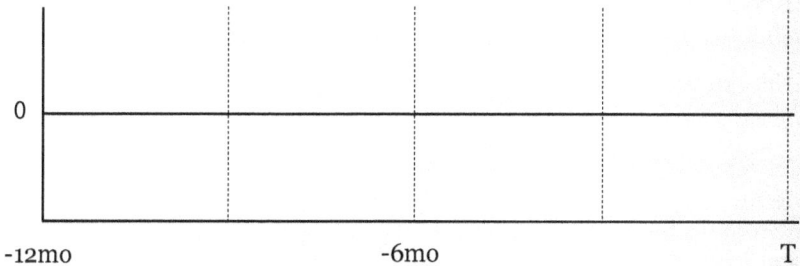

0

-12mo                              -6mo                              T

## quote/financial highlights

Stock Price: _____
EPS: _____
P/E: _____
Market Cap: _____
Div (Yield): _____
Debt/Equity: _____
EPS Growth: Pos ____ Neg ____

## quote/financial highlights

EBIT:     Pos ____ Neg ____
Assets:   Pos ____ Neg ____
LT Debt:  Pos ____ Neg ____

## value price

EPS*10: _____
EPS*15: _____
Book/Share: _____

## key ratios

| | Company | Industry |
|---|---|---|
| SG: Sales | _____ | _____ |
| G: Income | _____ | _____ |
| P: Price/Sales | _____ | _____ |
| P: Price/Book | _____ | _____ |
| P: Price/CF | _____ | _____ |
| M: Net | _____ | _____ |
| I: ROE | _____ | _____ |
| I: ROA | _____ | _____ |
| I: ROC | _____ | _____ |

## personal call

| price | bargain | fair | high | crazy | decision | buy | wait | ignore |
|---|---|---|---|---|---|---|---|---|

# Stock Tracker

Personal Investment Journal
by bookmark[pro]™

company .....................................................................................................................................................

industry ........................................................... industry leader ...........................................................

## key ratios: 10 yr comparisons

P/E: _____ > _____
P/S: _____ > _____
P/B: _____ > _____
Net Profit: _____ > _____
Book/Share: _____ > _____
ROE: _____ > _____
ROA: _____ > _____

## analyst ratings

| Strong Buy | | | Mod Buy |
|---|---|---|---|
| | Hold | | |
| Strong Sell | | | Mod Sell |
| | Buy | Sell | |
| Insiders | | | |

## sec filings (10K/10Q)

CEO: Name _____ Years _____ Prior _____
CFO: Name _____ Years _____ Prior _____
Rational: _____ Moat Size: _____
New Products or Acquisitions: _____

Competitive Advantage: _____
_____
_____

Profit Engine: _____
_____

## research

Company Web Site: _____
Wikipedia.org: _____
Google News: _____
CNBC.com: _____
Fortune.com: _____

BusinessWeek.com: _____

# Stock Tracker

company ............................................................ symbol .......... date ................

attention trigger ........................................................................................

.........................................................................................................................

## graph (1 year)

0 ─────────────────────────────────────────────

-12mo                  -6mo              T

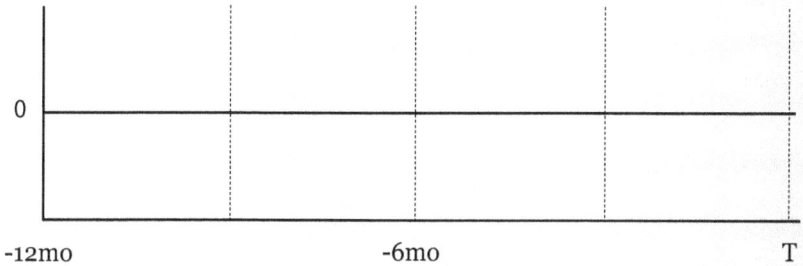

## quote/financial highlights

Stock Price: _____
EPS: _____
P/E: _____
Market Cap: _____
Div (Yield): _____
Debt/Equity: _____
EPS Growth: Pos ____ Neg ____

## quote/financial highlights

EBIT: Pos ____ Neg ____
Assets: Pos ____ Neg ____
LT Debt: Pos ____ Neg ____

## value price

EPS*10: _____
EPS*15: _____
Book/Share: _____

## key ratios

| | Company | Industry |
|---|---|---|
| SG: Sales | _____ | _____ |
| G: Income | _____ | _____ |
| P: Price/Sales | _____ | _____ |
| P: Price/Book | _____ | _____ |
| P: Price/CF | _____ | _____ |
| M: Net | _____ | _____ |
| I: ROE | _____ | _____ |
| I: ROA | _____ | _____ |
| I: ROC | _____ | _____ |

## personal call

| price | bargain | fair | high | crazy | decision | buy | wait | ignore |
|---|---|---|---|---|---|---|---|---|

# Stock Tracker

company ................................................................................................................

industry ......................................... industry leader ........................................

## key ratios: 10 yr comparisons

P/E:          _____ > _____
P/S:          _____ > _____
P/B:          _____ > _____
Net Profit:   _____ > _____
Book/Share: _____ > _____
ROE:          _____ > _____
ROA:          _____ > _____

## analyst ratings

| Strong Buy | | Mod Buy |
|---|---|---|
| | Hold | |
| Strong Sell | | Mod Sell |
| | Buy | Sell |
| Insiders | | |

## sec filings (10K/10Q)

CEO: Name_____ Years_____ Prior_____
CFO: Name_____ Years_____ Prior_____
Rational:_____ Moat Size: _____
New Products or Acquisitions:_____

Competitive Advantage:_____

Profit Engine:_____

## research

Company Web Site: _____
Wikipedia.org:      _____
Google News:        _____
CNBC.com:           _____
Fortune.com:        _____

BusinessWeek.com:_____

# Stock Tracker

Personal Investment Journal
by bookmark™

company ........................................................... symbol .......... date ...............

attention trigger ...........................................................................................

...................................................................................................................

## graph (1 year)

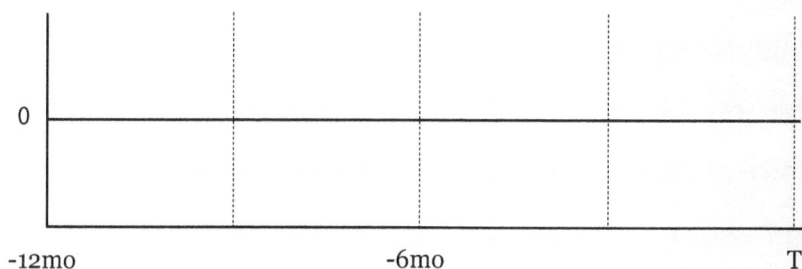

0

-12mo                          -6mo                                    T

## quote/financial highlights

Stock Price: _____

EPS: _____

P/E: _____

Market Cap: _____

Div (Yield): _____

Debt/Equity: _____

EPS Growth: Pos ___ Neg ___

## quote/financial highlights

EBIT:      Pos ___ Neg ___

Assets:    Pos ___ Neg ___

LT Debt:   Pos ___ Neg ___

## value price

EPS*10: _____

EPS*15: _____

Book/Share: _____

## key ratios      Company   Industry

SG: Sales       _____  _____

G: Income       _____  _____

P: Price/Sales  _____  _____

P: Price/Book   _____  _____

P: Price/CF     _____  _____

M: Net          _____  _____

I: ROE          _____  _____

I: ROA          _____  _____

I: ROC          _____  _____

## personal call

| price | bargain | fair | high | crazy | decision | buy | wait | ignore |

# **Stock Tracker**

Personal Investment Journal
by **bookmark**™

company ...........................................................................................................................

industry ........................................... industry leader .........................................

## key ratios: 10 yr comparisons

P/E: _____ > _____
P/S: _____ > _____
P/B: _____ > _____
Net Profit: _____ > _____
Book/Share: _____ > _____
ROE: _____ > _____
ROA: _____ > _____

## analyst ratings

| Strong Buy | | Mod Buy |
|---|---|---|
| | Hold | |
| Strong Sell | | Mod Sell |

| Buy | Sell |
|---|---|
| Insiders | |

## sec filings (10K/10Q)

CEO: Name _____ Years _____ Prior _____
CFO: Name _____ Years _____ Prior _____
Rational: _____ Moat Size: _____
New Products or Acquisitions: _____
_____
Competitive Advantage: _____
_____
_____
Profit Engine: _____
_____

## research

Company Web Site: _____
Wikipedia.org: _____
Google News: _____
CNBC.com: _____
Fortune.com: _____
BusinessWeek.com: _____

# Stock Tracker

company ............................................................... symbol .......... date ...............

attention trigger ...........................................................................

...................................................................................................

## graph (1 year)

0

-12mo    -6mo    T

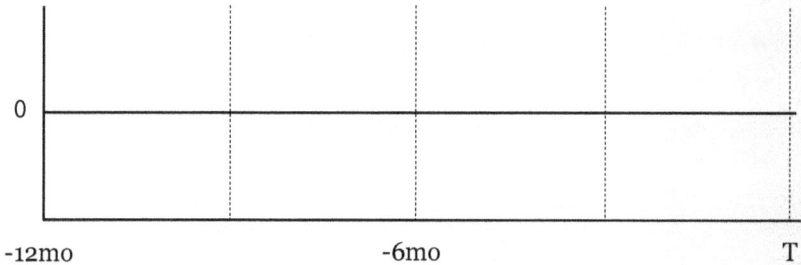

## quote/financial highlights

Stock Price: _____
EPS: _____
P/E: _____
Market Cap: _____
Div (Yield): _____
Debt/Equity: _____
EPS Growth: Pos ____ Neg ____

## quote/financial highlights

EBIT: Pos ____ Neg ____
Assets: Pos ____ Neg ____
LT Debt: Pos ____ Neg ____

## value price

EPS*10: _____
EPS*15: _____
Book/Share: _____

## key ratios

| | Company | Industry |
|---|---|---|
| SG: Sales | _____ | _____ |
| G: Income | _____ | _____ |
| P: Price/Sales | _____ | _____ |
| P: Price/Book | _____ | _____ |
| P: Price/CF | _____ | _____ |
| M: Net | _____ | _____ |
| I: ROE | _____ | _____ |
| I: ROA | _____ | _____ |
| I: ROC | _____ | _____ |

## personal call

| price | bargain | fair | high | crazy | decision | buy | wait | ignore |
|---|---|---|---|---|---|---|---|---|

# Stock Tracker

company ........................................................................................................

industry ...................................... industry leader ......................................

## key ratios: 10 yr comparisons

P/E: _____ > _____
P/S: _____ > _____
P/B: _____ > _____
Net Profit: _____ > _____
Book/Share: _____ > _____
ROE: _____ > _____
ROA: _____ > _____

## analyst ratings

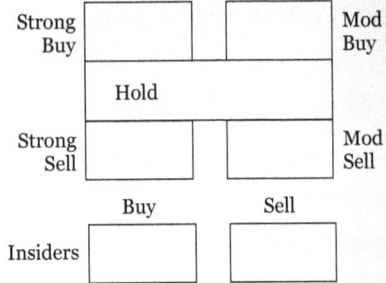

| | Strong Buy | | Mod Buy |
|---|---|---|---|
| | | Hold | |
| | Strong Sell | | Mod Sell |
| | Buy | Sell | |
| Insiders | | | |

## sec filings (10K/10Q)

CEO: Name _____ Years _____ Prior _____

CFO: Name _____ Years _____ Prior _____

Rational: _____ Moat Size: _____

New Products or Acquisitions: _____

_____

Competitive Advantage: _____

_____

_____

Profit Engine: _____

_____

## research

Company Web Site: _____

Wikipedia.org: _____

Google News: _____

CNBC.com: _____

Fortune.com: _____

BusinessWeek.com: _____

# Stock Tracker

company ............................................................ symbol .......... date ...............

attention trigger ..........................................................................................

..........................................................................................

## graph (1 year)

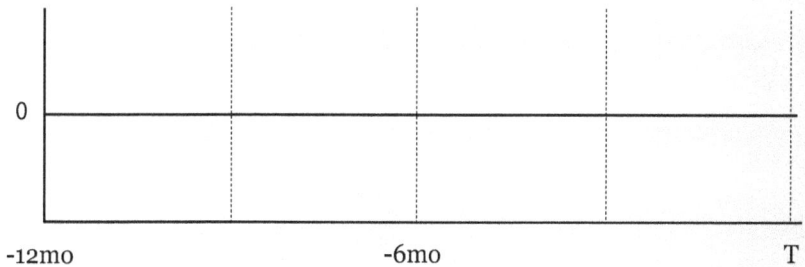

0

-12mo                  -6mo             T

## quote/financial highlights

Stock Price: _____

EPS: _____

P/E: _____

Market Cap: _____

Div (Yield): _____

Debt/Equity: _____

EPS Growth: Pos ____ Neg ____

## quote/financial highlights

EBIT:      Pos ____ Neg ____

Assets:      Pos ____ Neg ____

LT Debt:      Pos ____ Neg ____

## value price

EPS*10: _____

EPS*15: _____

Book/Share: _____

## key ratios

| | Company | Industry |
|---|---|---|
| SG: Sales | _____ | _____ |
| G: Income | _____ | _____ |
| P: Price/Sales | _____ | _____ |
| P: Price/Book | _____ | _____ |
| P: Price/CF | _____ | _____ |
| M: Net | _____ | _____ |
| I: ROE | _____ | _____ |
| I: ROA | _____ | _____ |
| I: ROC | _____ | _____ |

## personal call

| price | bargain | fair | high | crazy | | decision | buy | wait | ignore |
|---|---|---|---|---|---|---|---|---|---|

# Stock Tracker

company .......................................................................................................

industry ........................................ industry leader ...........................................

## key ratios: 10 yr comparisons

P/E:              _____ > _____
P/S:              _____ > _____
P/B:              _____ > _____
Net Profit:     _____ > _____
Book/Share: _____ > _____
ROE:             _____ > _____
ROA:             _____ > _____

## analyst ratings

| Strong Buy | | | Mod Buy |
|---|---|---|---|
| | Hold | | |
| Strong Sell | | | Mod Sell |
| | Buy | Sell | |
| Insiders | | | |

## sec filings (10K/10Q)

CEO: Name _____ Years _____ Prior _____
CFO: Name _____ Years _____ Prior _____
Rational: _____ Moat Size: _____
New Products or Acquisitions: _____
_____
Competitive Advantage: _____
_____
_____
Profit Engine: _____
_____

## research

Company Web Site: _____
Wikipedia.org:        _____
Google News:        _____
CNBC.com:            _____
Fortune.com:          _____
BusinessWeek.com: _____

# Stock Tracker

company ................................................................ symbol .......... date ..............

attention trigger ............................................................................................

................................................................................................................

## graph (1 year)

0 ————————————————————————————————

-12mo                    -6mo                            T

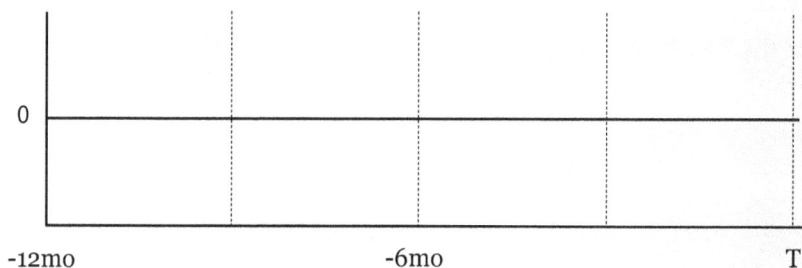

## quote/financial highlights

Stock Price: _____

EPS: _____

P/E: _____

Market Cap: _____

Div (Yield): _____

Debt/Equity: _____

EPS Growth: Pos ___ Neg ___

## quote/financial highlights

EBIT:        Pos ___ Neg ___

Assets:      Pos ___ Neg ___

LT Debt:     Pos ___ Neg ___

## value price

EPS*10: _____

EPS*15: _____

Book/Share: _____

## key ratios

| | Company | Industry |
|---|---|---|
| SG: Sales | ___ | ___ |
| G: Income | ___ | ___ |
| P: Price/Sales | ___ | ___ |
| P: Price/Book | ___ | ___ |
| P: Price/CF | ___ | ___ |
| M: Net | ___ | ___ |
| I: ROE | ___ | ___ |
| I: ROA | ___ | ___ |
| I: ROC | ___ | ___ |

## personal call

| price | bargain | fair | high | crazy | | decision | buy | wait | ignore |
|---|---|---|---|---|---|---|---|---|---|

# Stock Tracker

Personal Investment Journal
by bookmark™

company .................................................................................................................

industry ........................................ industry leader ......................................

## key ratios: 10 yr comparisons

P/E:          _____ > _____
P/S:          _____ > _____
P/B:          _____ > _____
Net Profit:   _____ > _____
Book/Share:  _____ > _____
ROE:          _____ > _____
ROA:          _____ > _____

## analyst ratings

| Strong Buy | | | Mod Buy |
|---|---|---|---|
| | Hold | | |
| Strong Sell | | | Mod Sell |
| | Buy | Sell | |
| Insiders | | | |

## sec filings (10K/10Q)

CEO: Name _____ Years _____ Prior _____
CFO: Name _____ Years _____ Prior _____
Rational: _____ Moat Size: _____
New Products or Acquisitions: _____
_____
Competitive Advantage: _____
_____
_____
Profit Engine: _____
_____

## research

Company Web Site: _____
Wikipedia.org:      _____
Google News:        _____
CNBC.com:           _____
Fortune.com:        _____
BusinessWeek.com: _____

# Stock Tracker

company ............................................................ symbol ......... date ...............

attention trigger .........................................................................................

.....................................................................................................................

---

graph (1 year)

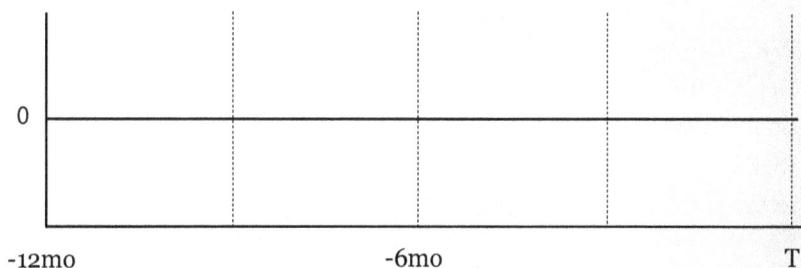

0

-12mo                    -6mo                              T

---

## quote/financial highlights

Stock Price: _____
EPS:         _____
P/E:         _____
Market Cap:  _____
Div (Yield): _____
Debt/Equity: _____
EPS Growth: Pos ____ Neg ____

## quote/financial highlights

EBIT:    Pos ____ Neg ____
Assets:  Pos ____ Neg ____
LT Debt: Pos ____ Neg ____

## value price

EPS*10:      _____
EPS*15:      _____
Book/Share:  _____

## key ratios

| key ratios | Company | Industry |
|---|---|---|
| SG: Sales | ____ | ____ |
| G: Income | ____ | ____ |
| P: Price/Sales | ____ | ____ |
| P: Price/Book | ____ | ____ |
| P: Price/CF | ____ | ____ |
| M: Net | ____ | ____ |
| I: ROE | ____ | ____ |
| I: ROA | ____ | ____ |
| I: ROC | ____ | ____ |

---

## personal call

| price | bargain | fair | high | crazy | decision | buy | wait | ignore |
|---|---|---|---|---|---|---|---|---|

# Stock Tracker

company ..............................................................................................................................

industry ............................................... industry leader .......................................

## key ratios: 10 yr comparisons

P/E: _____ > _____
P/S: _____ > _____
P/B: _____ > _____
Net Profit: _____ > _____
Book/Share: _____ > _____
ROE: _____ > _____
ROA: _____ > _____

## analyst ratings

| Strong Buy | | | Mod Buy |
|---|---|---|---|
| | Hold | | |
| Strong Sell | | | Mod Sell |
| | Buy | Sell | |
| Insiders | | | |

## sec filings (10K/10Q)

CEO: Name _____ Years _____ Prior _____

CFO: Name _____ Years _____ Prior _____

Rational: _____ Moat Size: _____

New Products or Acquisitions: _____

_____

Competitive Advantage: _____

_____

_____

Profit Engine: _____

_____

## research

Company Web Site: _____

Wikipedia.org: _____

Google News: _____

CNBC.com: _____

Fortune.com: _____

BusinessWeek.com: _____

# Stock Tracker

Personal Investment Journal
by bookmark™

company ............................................................ symbol .......... date ...............

attention trigger ...........................................................................................

...........................................................................................

## graph (1 year)

0

-12mo                          -6mo                          T

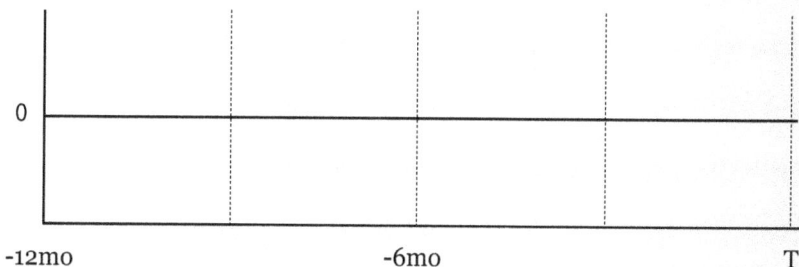

## quote/financial highlights

Stock Price: _____
EPS: _____
P/E: _____
Market Cap: _____
Div (Yield): _____
Debt/Equity: _____
EPS Growth: Pos ____ Neg ____

## quote/financial highlights

EBIT:      Pos ____ Neg ____
Assets:    Pos ____ Neg ____
LT Debt:   Pos ____ Neg ____

## value price

EPS*10: _____
EPS*15: _____
Book/Share: _____

## key ratios

| | Company | Industry |
| --- | --- | --- |
| SG: Sales | _____ | _____ |
| G: Income | _____ | _____ |
| P: Price/Sales | _____ | _____ |
| P: Price/Book | _____ | _____ |
| P: Price/CF | _____ | _____ |
| M: Net | _____ | _____ |
| I: ROE | _____ | _____ |
| I: ROA | _____ | _____ |
| I: ROC | _____ | _____ |

## personal call

| price | bargain | fair | high | crazy | decision | buy | wait | ignore |
| --- | --- | --- | --- | --- | --- | --- | --- | --- |

# Stock Tracker

company .......................................................................................................................

industry .............................................. industry leader .........................................

## key ratios: 10 yr comparisons

P/E:            _____ > _____
P/S:            _____ > _____
P/B:            _____ > _____
Net Profit:     _____ > _____
Book/Share:   _____ > _____
ROE:            _____ > _____
ROA:            _____ > _____

## analyst ratings

| Strong Buy | | Mod Buy |
| --- | --- | --- |
| | Hold | |
| Strong Sell | | Mod Sell |
| | Buy | Sell |
| Insiders | | |

## sec filings (10K/10Q)

CEO: Name _____ Years _____ Prior _____
CFO: Name _____ Years _____ Prior _____
Rational: _____ Moat Size: _____
New Products or Acquisitions: _____
_____
Competitive Advantage: _____
_____
_____
Profit Engine: _____
_____

## research

Company Web Site: _____
Wikipedia.org:      _____
Google News:        _____
CNBC.com:           _____
Fortune.com:        _____
BusinessWeek.com: _____

## Stock Tracker

company ........................................................ symbol ........ date ..............

attention trigger ........................................................................

........................................................................

### graph (1 year)

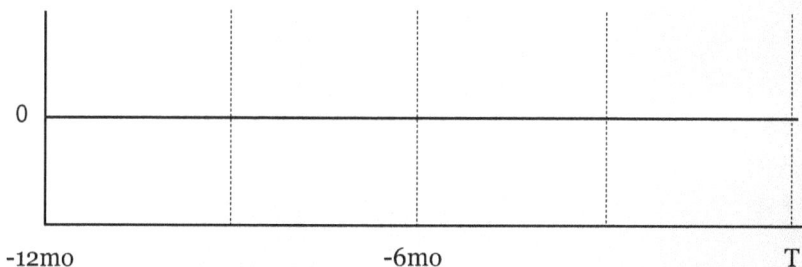

0

-12mo          -6mo          T

### quote/financial highlights

Stock Price: _____
EPS: _____
P/E: _____
Market Cap: _____
Div (Yield): _____
Debt/Equity: _____
EPS Growth: Pos ____ Neg ____

### quote/financial highlights

EBIT:      Pos ____ Neg ____
Assets:    Pos ____ Neg ____
LT Debt:   Pos ____ Neg ____

### value price

EPS*10:    _____
EPS*15:    _____
Book/Share: _____

### key ratios

| key ratios | Company | Industry |
|---|---|---|
| SG: Sales | _____ | _____ |
| G: Income | _____ | _____ |
| P: Price/Sales | _____ | _____ |
| P: Price/Book | _____ | _____ |
| P: Price/CF | _____ | _____ |
| M: Net | _____ | _____ |
| I: ROE | _____ | _____ |
| I: ROA | _____ | _____ |
| I: ROC | _____ | _____ |

### personal call

| price | bargain | fair | high | crazy | decision | buy | wait | ignore |

# Stock Tracker

company .........................................................................................................

industry ........................................... industry leader ...........................................

## key ratios: 10 yr comparisons

P/E: _____ > _____
P/S: _____ > _____
P/B: _____ > _____
Net Profit: _____ > _____
Book/Share: _____ > _____
ROE: _____ > _____
ROA: _____ > _____

## analyst ratings

Strong Buy | | | Mod Buy
Hold
Strong Sell | | | Mod Sell
Buy | Sell
Insiders | |

## sec filings (10K/10Q)

CEO: Name _____ Years _____ Prior _____
CFO: Name _____ Years _____ Prior _____
Rational: _____ Moat Size: _____
New Products or Acquisitions: _____
_____
Competitive Advantage: _____
_____
_____
Profit Engine: _____
_____

## research

Company Web Site: _____
Wikipedia.org: _____
Google News: _____
CNBC.com: _____
Fortune.com: _____
BusinessWeek.com: _____

# Stock Tracker

company ............................................................ symbol .......... date ...............

attention trigger ...............................................................................

........................................................................................................

## graph (1 year)

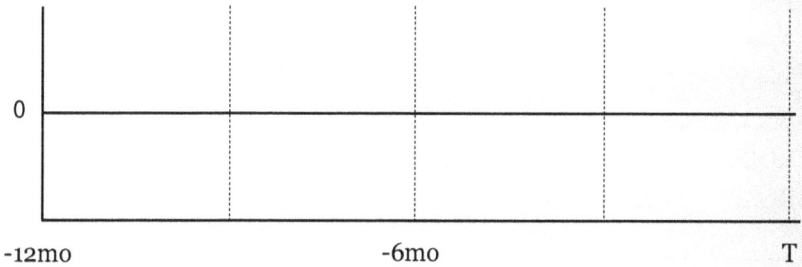

0

-12mo                    -6mo                                    T

## quote/financial highlights

Stock Price: _____
EPS: _____
P/E: _____
Market Cap: _____
Div (Yield): _____
Debt/Equity: _____
EPS Growth: Pos ____ Neg ____

## quote/financial highlights

EBIT:      Pos ____ Neg ____
Assets:    Pos ____ Neg ____
LT Debt:   Pos ____ Neg ____

## value price

EPS*10: _____
EPS*15: _____
Book/Share: _____

## key ratios

| | Company | Industry |
|---|---|---|
| SG: Sales | _____ | _____ |
| G: Income | _____ | _____ |
| P: Price/Sales | _____ | _____ |
| P: Price/Book | _____ | _____ |
| P: Price/CF | _____ | _____ |
| M: Net | _____ | _____ |
| I: ROE | _____ | _____ |
| I: ROA | _____ | _____ |
| I: ROC | _____ | _____ |

## personal call

| price | bargain | fair | high | crazy | decision | buy | wait | ignore |
|---|---|---|---|---|---|---|---|---|

# Stock Tracker

company .................................................................................................................

industry ............................................. industry leader ...........................................

## key ratios: 10 yr comparisons

P/E: _____ > _____
P/S: _____ > _____
P/B: _____ > _____
Net Profit: _____ > _____
Book/Share: _____ > _____
ROE: _____ > _____
ROA: _____ > _____

## analyst ratings

| Strong Buy | | | Mod Buy |
|---|---|---|---|
| | Hold | | |
| Strong Sell | | | Mod Sell |
| | Buy | Sell | |
| Insiders | | | |

## sec filings (10K/10Q)

CEO: Name _____ Years _____ Prior _____
CFO: Name _____ Years _____ Prior _____
Rational: _____ Moat Size: _____
New Products or Acquisitions: _____

Competitive Advantage: _____

Profit Engine: _____

## research

Company Web Site: _____
Wikipedia.org: _____
Google News: _____
CNBC.com: _____
Fortune.com: _____

BusinessWeek.com: _____

# Stock Tracker

company ........................................................... symbol ........ date ...........

attention trigger ...................................................................

..................................................................................................

## graph (1 year)

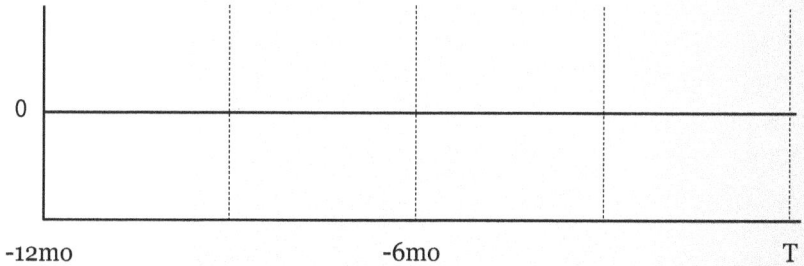

0

-12mo                    -6mo                         T

## quote/financial highlights

Stock Price: _____

EPS: _____

P/E: _____

Market Cap: _____

Div (Yield): _____

Debt/Equity: _____

EPS Growth: Pos ____ Neg ____

## quote/financial highlights

EBIT:     Pos ____ Neg ____

Assets:   Pos ____ Neg ____

LT Debt:  Pos ____ Neg ____

## value price

EPS*10: _____

EPS*15: _____

Book/Share: _____

## key ratios

| | Company | Industry |
| --- | --- | --- |
| SG: Sales | | |
| G: Income | | |
| P: Price/Sales | | |
| P: Price/Book | | |
| P: Price/CF | | |
| M: Net | | |
| I: ROE | | |
| I: ROA | | |
| I: ROC | | |

## personal call

price | bargain | fair | high | crazy |   decision | buy | wait | ignore

# Stock Tracker

Personal Investment Journal
by pro bookmark™

company .................................................................................................................

industry ............................................ industry leader ..............................................

## key ratios: 10 yr comparisons

P/E: _____ > _____
P/S: _____ > _____
P/B: _____ > _____
Net Profit: _____ > _____
Book/Share: _____ > _____
ROE: _____ > _____
ROA: _____ > _____

## analyst ratings

| | Strong Buy | | Mod Buy |
|---|---|---|---|
| | | Hold | |
| | Strong Sell | | Mod Sell |
| Insiders | Buy | Sell | |

## sec filings (10K/10Q)

CEO: Name _____ Years _____ Prior _____
CFO: Name _____ Years _____ Prior _____
Rational: _____ Moat Size: _____
New Products or Acquisitions: _____
_____

Competitive Advantage: _____
_____
_____

Profit Engine: _____
_____

## research

Company Web Site: _____
Wikipedia.org: _____
Google News: _____
CNBC.com: _____
Fortune.com: _____
BusinessWeek.com: _____

# Stock Tracker

company ............................................................ symbol ......... date ..............

attention trigger ..................................................................................

....................................................................................................

## graph (1 year)

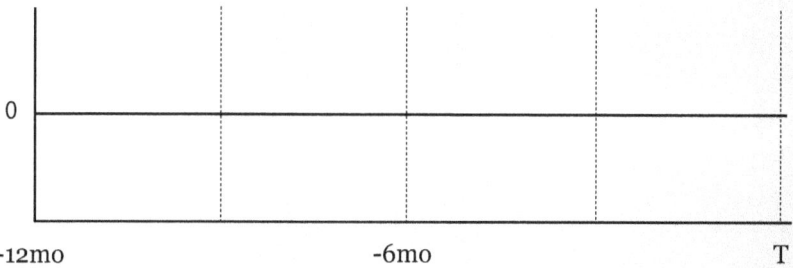

0

-12mo          -6mo          T

## quote/financial highlights

Stock Price: _____
EPS: _____
P/E: _____
Market Cap: _____
Div (Yield): _____
Debt/Equity: _____
EPS Growth: Pos ____ Neg ____

## quote/financial highlights

EBIT:     Pos ____ Neg ____
Assets:   Pos ____ Neg ____
LT Debt:  Pos ____ Neg ____

## value price

EPS*10: _____
EPS*15: _____
Book/Share: _____

## key ratios

| | Company | Industry |
|---|---|---|
| SG: Sales | ____ | ____ |
| G: Income | ____ | ____ |
| P: Price/Sales | ____ | ____ |
| P: Price/Book | ____ | ____ |
| P: Price/CF | ____ | ____ |
| M: Net | ____ | ____ |
| I: ROE | ____ | ____ |
| I: ROA | ____ | ____ |
| I: ROC | ____ | ____ |

## personal call

price | bargain | fair | high | crazy     decision | buy | wait | ignore

# Stock Tracker

company .................................................................................................................

industry .......................................... industry leader .........................................

## key ratios: 10 yr comparisons

P/E: _____ > _____
P/S: _____ > _____
P/B: _____ > _____
Net Profit: _____ > _____
Book/Share: _____ > _____
ROE: _____ > _____
ROA: _____ > _____

## analyst ratings

| Strong Buy | | | Mod Buy |
|---|---|---|---|
| | Hold | | |
| Strong Sell | | | Mod Sell |
| | Buy | Sell | |
| Insiders | | | |

## sec filings (10K/10Q)

CEO: Name _____ Years _____ Prior _____
CFO: Name _____ Years _____ Prior _____
Rational: _____ Moat Size: _____
New Products or Acquisitions: _____
_____
Competitive Advantage: _____
_____
_____
Profit Engine: _____
_____

## research

Company Web Site: _____
Wikipedia.org: _____
Google News: _____
CNBC.com: _____
Fortune.com: _____
BusinessWeek.com: _____

# Stock Tracker

company ............................................................... symbol .......... date ...............

attention trigger ...........................................................................

...................................................................................................

## graph (1 year)

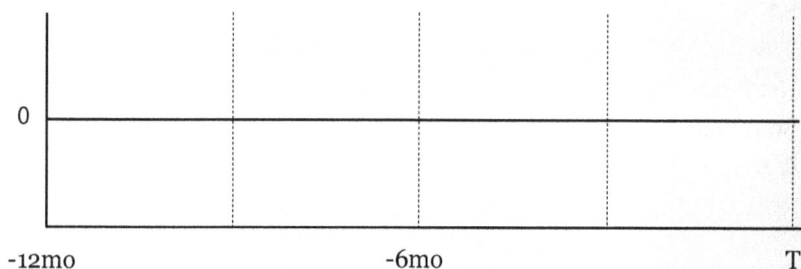

0

-12mo                    -6mo                              T

## quote/financial highlights

Stock Price: _____
EPS: _____
P/E: _____
Market Cap: _____
Div (Yield): _____
Debt/Equity: _____
EPS Growth: Pos _____ Neg _____

## quote/financial highlights

EBIT:      Pos _____ Neg _____
Assets:    Pos _____ Neg _____
LT Debt:   Pos _____ Neg _____

## value price

EPS*10: _____
EPS*15: _____
Book/Share: _____

## key ratios

| | Company | Industry |
|---|---|---|
| SG: Sales | _____ | _____ |
| G: Income | _____ | _____ |
| P: Price/Sales | _____ | _____ |
| P: Price/Book | _____ | _____ |
| P: Price/CF | _____ | _____ |
| M: Net | _____ | _____ |
| I: ROE | _____ | _____ |
| I: ROA | _____ | _____ |
| I: ROC | _____ | _____ |

## personal call

| price | bargain | fair | high | crazy | decision | buy | wait | ignore |
|---|---|---|---|---|---|---|---|---|

85

# Stock Tracker

company ................................................................................................................

industry ................................................ industry leader ................................................

## key ratios: 10 yr comparisons

P/E:  _____ > _____
P/S:  _____ > _____
P/B:  _____ > _____
Net Profit:  _____ > _____
Book/Share:  _____ > _____
ROE:  _____ > _____
ROA:  _____ > _____

## analyst ratings

| Strong Buy | | | Mod Buy |
| Hold | | | |
| Strong Sell | | | Mod Sell |
| Buy | | Sell | |
| Insiders | | | |

## sec filings (10K/10Q)

CEO: Name _____ Years _____ Prior _____
CFO: Name _____ Years _____ Prior _____
Rational: _____ Moat Size: _____
New Products or Acquisitions: _____
_____

Competitive Advantage: _____
_____
_____

Profit Engine: _____
_____

## research

Company Web Site: _____
Wikipedia.org:    _____
Google News:      _____
CNBC.com:         _____
Fortune.com:      _____
BusinessWeek.com: _____

# Stock Tracker

company .............................................................. symbol .......... date ...............

attention trigger ........................................................................................

..............................................................................................................

## graph (1 year)

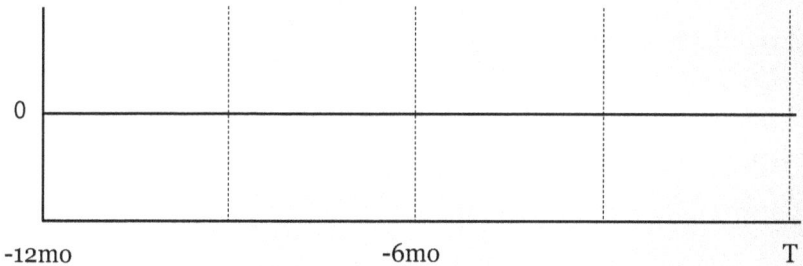

0

-12mo                              -6mo                              T

## quote/financial highlights

Stock Price: _____
EPS: _____
P/E: _____
Market Cap: _____
Div (Yield): _____
Debt/Equity: _____
EPS Growth: Pos ____ Neg ____

## quote/financial highlights

EBIT:        Pos ____ Neg ____
Assets:      Pos ____ Neg ____
LT Debt:     Pos ____ Neg ____

## value price

EPS*10: _____
EPS*15: _____
Book/Share: _____

## key ratios        Company   Industry

| | Company | Industry |
|---|---|---|
| SG: Sales | _____ | _____ |
| G: Income | _____ | _____ |
| P: Price/Sales | _____ | _____ |
| P: Price/Book | _____ | _____ |
| P: Price/CF | _____ | _____ |
| M: Net | _____ | _____ |
| I: ROE | _____ | _____ |
| I: ROA | _____ | _____ |
| I: ROC | _____ | _____ |

## personal call

| price | bargain | fair | high | crazy | decision | buy | wait | ignore |

# Stock Tracker

company ...........................................................................................................

industry .......................................... industry leader ........................................

## key ratios: 10 yr comparisons

P/E: _____ > _____
P/S: _____ > _____
P/B: _____ > _____
Net Profit: _____ > _____
Book/Share: _____ > _____
ROE: _____ > _____
ROA: _____ > _____

## analyst ratings

| | Strong Buy | | Mod Buy | |
|---|---|---|---|---|
| Strong Buy | | | | Mod Buy |
| | Hold | | | |
| Strong Sell | | | | Mod Sell |
| | Buy | Sell | | |
| Insiders | | | | |

## sec filings (10K/10Q)

CEO: Name _____ Years _____ Prior _____
CFO: Name _____ Years _____ Prior _____
Rational: _____ Moat Size: _____
New Products or Acquisitions: _____
_____
Competitive Advantage: _____
_____
_____
Profit Engine: _____
_____

## research

Company Web Site: _____
Wikipedia.org: _____
Google News: _____
CNBC.com: _____
Fortune.com: _____
BusinessWeek.com: _____

# Stock Tracker

company ................................................. symbol .......... date ..............

attention trigger ....................................................................

........................................................................................

## graph (1 year)

0 ——————————————————————————————

-12mo                    -6mo                         T

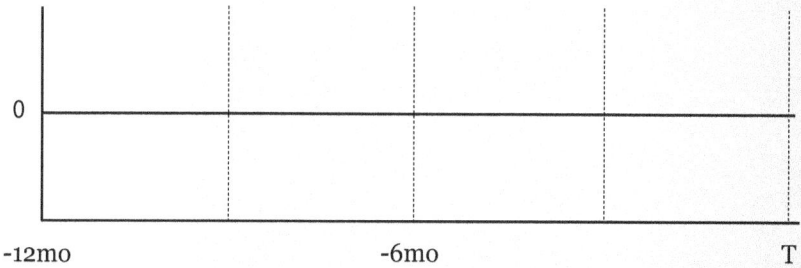

## quote/financial highlights

Stock Price: _____
EPS:             _____
P/E:             _____
Market Cap: _____
Div (Yield):  _____
Debt/Equity: _____
EPS Growth: Pos ____ Neg ____

## quote/financial highlights

EBIT:      Pos ____ Neg ____
Assets:   Pos ____ Neg ____
LT Debt: Pos ____ Neg ____

## value price

EPS*10:        _____
EPS*15:        _____
Book/Share: _____

## key ratios

| | Company | Industry |
|---|---|---|
| SG: Sales | | |
| G: Income | | |
| P: Price/Sales | | |
| P: Price/Book | | |
| P: Price/CF | | |
| M: Net | | |
| I: ROE | | |
| I: ROA | | |
| I: ROC | | |

## personal call

| price | bargain | fair | high | crazy | decision | buy | wait | ignore |
|---|---|---|---|---|---|---|---|---|

89

# Stock Tracker

company ...........................................................................................................................

industry ......................................... industry leader .........................................

## key ratios: 10 yr comparisons

P/E:            _____ > _____
P/S:            _____ > _____
P/B:            _____ > _____
Net Profit:   _____ > _____
Book/Share: _____ > _____
ROE:           _____ > _____
ROA:           _____ > _____

## analyst ratings

| Strong Buy | | | Mod Buy |
| Hold | | | |
| Strong Sell | | | Mod Sell |
| Insiders | Buy | Sell | |

## sec filings (10K/10Q)

CEO: Name _____ Years _____ Prior _____
CFO: Name _____ Years _____ Prior _____
Rational: _____ Moat Size: _____
New Products or Acquisitions: _____
_____
Competitive Advantage: _____
_____
_____
Profit Engine: _____
_____

## research

Company Web Site: _____
Wikipedia.org:       _____
Google News:        _____
CNBC.com:            _____
Fortune.com:         _____
BusinessWeek.com: _____

# Stock Tracker

company ............................................................ symbol .......... date ................

attention trigger ..........................................................................................

..........................................................................................

## graph (1 year)

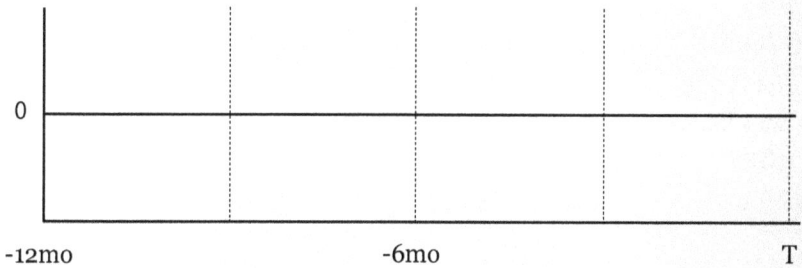

0 _____

-12mo              -6mo            T

## quote/financial highlights

Stock Price: _____
EPS: _____
P/E: _____
Market Cap: _____
Div (Yield): _____
Debt/Equity: _____
EPS Growth: Pos ____ Neg ____

## quote/financial highlights

EBIT:     Pos ____ Neg ____
Assets:   Pos ____ Neg ____
LT Debt:  Pos ____ Neg ____

## value price

EPS*10: _____
EPS*15: _____
Book/Share: _____

## key ratios

| | Company | Industry |
|---|---|---|
| SG: Sales | _____ | _____ |
| G: Income | _____ | _____ |
| P: Price/Sales | _____ | _____ |
| P: Price/Book | _____ | _____ |
| P: Price/CF | _____ | _____ |
| M: Net | _____ | _____ |
| I: ROE | _____ | _____ |
| I: ROA | _____ | _____ |
| I: ROC | _____ | _____ |

## personal call

| price | bargain | fair | high | crazy | decision | buy | wait | ignore |

# Stock Tracker

company .........................................................................................................................

industry ........................................... industry leader .........................................

## key ratios: 10 yr comparisons

P/E:              _____ > _____
P/S:              _____ > _____
P/B:              _____ > _____
Net Profit:       _____ > _____
Book/Share:       _____ > _____
ROE:              _____ > _____
ROA:              _____ > _____

## analyst ratings

| | Strong Buy | | | Mod Buy |
| Hold | | | |
| | Strong Sell | | | Mod Sell |
| | Buy | | Sell | |
| Insiders | | | |

## sec filings (10K/10Q)

CEO: Name _____ Years _____ Prior _____

CFO: Name _____ Years _____ Prior _____

Rational:_____ Moat Size: _____

New Products or Acquisitions:_____

_____

Competitive Advantage:_____

_____

_____

Profit Engine:_____

_____

## research

Company Web Site: _____

Wikipedia.org:      _____

Google News:        _____

CNBC.com:           _____

Fortune.com:        _____

BusinessWeek.com:_____

# Stock Tracker

company ................................................................. symbol .......... date ................

attention trigger ........................................................................................

........................................................................................................................

## graph (1 year)

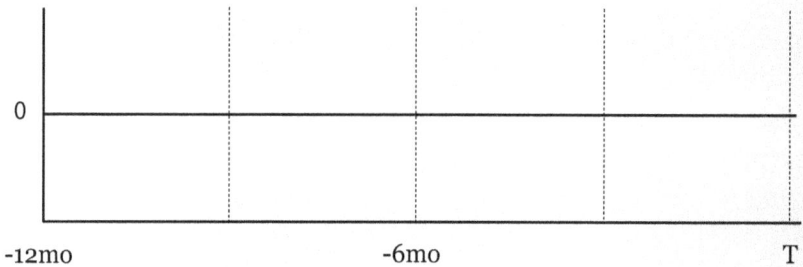

0

-12mo                          -6mo                                        T

## quote/financial highlights

Stock Price: _____

EPS: _____

P/E: _____

Market Cap: _____

Div (Yield): _____

Debt/Equity: _____

EPS Growth: Pos ____ Neg ____

## quote/financial highlights

EBIT:        Pos ____ Neg ____

Assets:      Pos ____ Neg ____

LT Debt:     Pos ____ Neg ____

## value price

EPS*10: _____

EPS*15: _____

Book/Share: _____

## key ratios

| | Company | Industry |
|---|---|---|
| SG: Sales | _____ | _____ |
| G: Income | _____ | _____ |
| P: Price/Sales | _____ | _____ |
| P: Price/Book | _____ | _____ |
| P: Price/CF | _____ | _____ |
| M: Net | _____ | _____ |
| I: ROE | _____ | _____ |
| I: ROA | _____ | _____ |
| I: ROC | _____ | _____ |

## personal call

| price | bargain | fair | high | crazy | decision | buy | wait | ignore |
|---|---|---|---|---|---|---|---|---|

# Stock Tracker

company .......................................................................................................

industry .......................................... industry leader ..................................

## key ratios: 10 yr comparisons

P/E:            _____ > _____
P/S:            _____ > _____
P/B:            _____ > _____
Net Profit:     _____ > _____
Book/Share: _____ > _____
ROE:            _____ > _____
ROA:            _____ > _____

## analyst ratings

| Strong Buy | | | Mod Buy |
| Hold | | | |
| Strong Sell | | | Mod Sell |
| Insiders | Buy | Sell | |

## sec filings (10K/10Q)

CEO: Name _____ Years _____ Prior _____
CFO: Name _____ Years _____ Prior _____
Rational: _____ Moat Size: _____
New Products or Acquisitions: _____
_____
Competitive Advantage: _____
_____
_____
Profit Engine: _____
_____

## research

Company Web Site: _____
Wikipedia.org:     _____
Google News:       _____
CNBC.com:          _____
Fortune.com:       _____
BusinessWeek.com: _____

# Stock Tracker

company ............................................................... symbol .......... date ................

attention trigger ...........................................................................................

.........................................................................................................................

## graph (1 year)

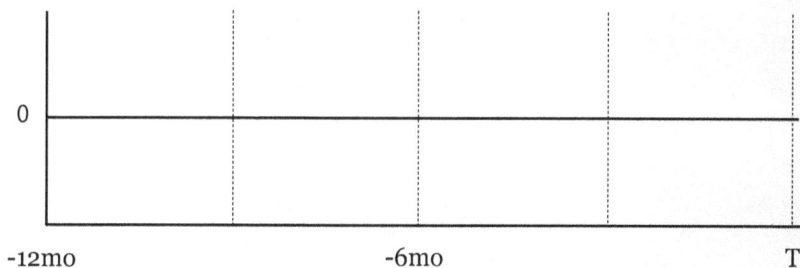

0

-12mo                      -6mo                                        T

## quote/financial highlights

Stock Price: _____

EPS: _____

P/E: _____

Market Cap: _____

Div (Yield): _____

Debt/Equity: _____

EPS Growth: Pos _____ Neg _____

## quote/financial highlights

EBIT:       Pos _____ Neg _____

Assets:     Pos _____ Neg _____

LT Debt:    Pos _____ Neg _____

## value price

EPS*10: _____

EPS*15: _____

Book/Share: _____

## key ratios

| | Company | Industry |
|---|---|---|
| SG: Sales | _____ | _____ |
| G: Income | _____ | _____ |
| P: Price/Sales | _____ | _____ |
| P: Price/Book | _____ | _____ |
| P: Price/CF | _____ | _____ |
| M: Net | _____ | _____ |
| I: ROE | _____ | _____ |
| I: ROA | _____ | _____ |
| I: ROC | _____ | _____ |

## personal call

| price | bargain | fair | high | crazy | decision | buy | wait | ignore |
|---|---|---|---|---|---|---|---|---|

95

# Stock Tracker

company .............................................................................................................

industry ........................................... industry leader .......................................

## key ratios: 10 yr comparisons

P/E:  _____ > _____
P/S:  _____ > _____
P/B:  _____ > _____
Net Profit:  _____ > _____
Book/Share: _____ > _____
ROE:  _____ > _____
ROA:  _____ > _____

## analyst ratings

|  | Strong Buy |  | Mod Buy |
|--|--|--|--|
|  | Hold |  |  |
|  | Strong Sell |  | Mod Sell |
|  | Buy | Sell |  |
| Insiders |  |  |  |

## sec filings (10K/10Q)

CEO: Name _____ Years _____ Prior _____
CFO: Name _____ Years _____ Prior _____
Rational: _____ Moat Size: _____
New Products or Acquisitions: _____
_____
Competitive Advantage: _____
_____
_____
Profit Engine: _____
_____

## research

Company Web Site: _____
Wikipedia.org:    _____
Google News:      _____
CNBC.com:         _____
Fortune.com:      _____
BusinessWeek.com: _____

# Stock Tracker

company ............................................................ symbol ......... date ...............

attention trigger ..........................................................................................

..........................................................................................................................

## graph (1 year)

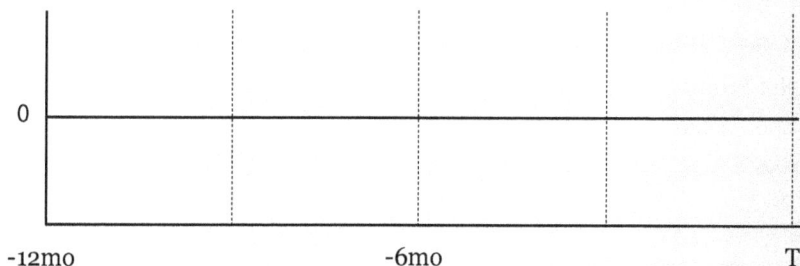

0

-12mo                    -6mo                              T

## quote/financial highlights

Stock Price: _____

EPS: _____

P/E: _____

Market Cap: _____

Div (Yield): _____

Debt/Equity: _____

EPS Growth: Pos ____ Neg ____

## quote/financial highlights

EBIT:     Pos ____ Neg ____

Assets:   Pos ____ Neg ____

LT Debt:  Pos ____ Neg ____

## value price

EPS*10: _____

EPS*15: _____

Book/Share: _____

## key ratios

| | Company | Industry |
|---|---|---|
| SG: Sales | _____ | _____ |
| G: Income | _____ | _____ |
| P: Price/Sales | _____ | _____ |
| P: Price/Book | _____ | _____ |
| P: Price/CF | _____ | _____ |
| M: Net | _____ | _____ |
| I: ROE | _____ | _____ |
| I: ROA | _____ | _____ |
| I: ROC | _____ | _____ |

## personal call

| price | bargain | fair | high | crazy | decision | buy | wait | ignore |
|---|---|---|---|---|---|---|---|---|

# Stock Tracker

company ...........................................................................................................

industry .......................................... industry leader ....................................

## key ratios: 10 yr comparisons

P/E: _____ > _____
P/S: _____ > _____
P/B: _____ > _____
Net Profit: _____ > _____
Book/Share: _____ > _____
ROE: _____ > _____
ROA: _____ > _____

## analyst ratings

| Strong Buy | | | Mod Buy |
|---|---|---|---|
| | Hold | | |
| Strong Sell | | | Mod Sell |
| | Buy | Sell | |
| Insiders | | | |

## sec filings (10K/10Q)

CEO: Name _____ Years _____ Prior_____
CFO: Name _____ Years _____ Prior_____
Rational:_____ Moat Size: _____
New Products or Acquisitions:_____

_____

Competitive Advantage:_____

_____

_____

Profit Engine:_____

_____

## research

Company Web Site: _____
Wikipedia.org: _____
Google News: _____
CNBC.com: _____
Fortune.com: _____

BusinessWeek.com:_____

# Stock Tracker

company ........................................................ symbol ......... date ...............

attention trigger ....................................................................................

........................................................................................................

## graph (1 year)

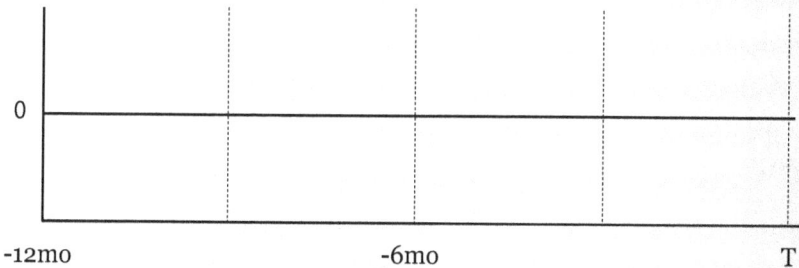

0

-12mo          -6mo          T

## quote/financial highlights

Stock Price: _____
EPS: _____
P/E: _____
Market Cap: _____
Div (Yield): _____
Debt/Equity: _____
EPS Growth: Pos ____ Neg ____

## quote/financial highlights

EBIT:     Pos ____ Neg ____
Assets:   Pos ____ Neg ____
LT Debt:  Pos ____ Neg ____

## value price

EPS*10: _____
EPS*15: _____
Book/Share: _____

## key ratios

| | Company | Industry |
|---|---|---|
| SG: Sales | _____ | _____ |
| G: Income | _____ | _____ |
| P: Price/Sales | _____ | _____ |
| P: Price/Book | _____ | _____ |
| P: Price/CF | _____ | _____ |
| M: Net | _____ | _____ |
| I: ROE | _____ | _____ |
| I: ROA | _____ | _____ |
| I: ROC | _____ | _____ |

## personal call

| price | bargain | fair | high | crazy | decision | buy | wait | ignore |

# Stock Tracker

company .......................................................................................................................

industry ........................................... industry leader ...........................................

## key ratios: 10 yr comparisons

P/E: _____ > _____
P/S: _____ > _____
P/B: _____ > _____
Net Profit: _____ > _____
Book/Share: _____ > _____
ROE: _____ > _____
ROA: _____ > _____

## analyst ratings

| Strong Buy | | Mod Buy |
| --- | --- | --- |
| | Hold | |
| Strong Sell | | Mod Sell |
| | Buy | Sell |
| Insiders | | |

## sec filings (10K/10Q)

CEO: Name _____ Years _____ Prior _____
CFO: Name _____ Years _____ Prior _____
Rational: _____ Moat Size: _____
New Products or Acquisitions: _____
_____
Competitive Advantage: _____
_____
_____
Profit Engine: _____
_____

## research

Company Web Site: _____
Wikipedia.org: _____
Google News: _____
CNBC.com: _____
Fortune.com: _____
BusinessWeek.com: _____

# Stock Tracker

company ................................................................ symbol .......... date ................

attention trigger ...............................................................................................

..........................................................................................................................

## graph (1 year)

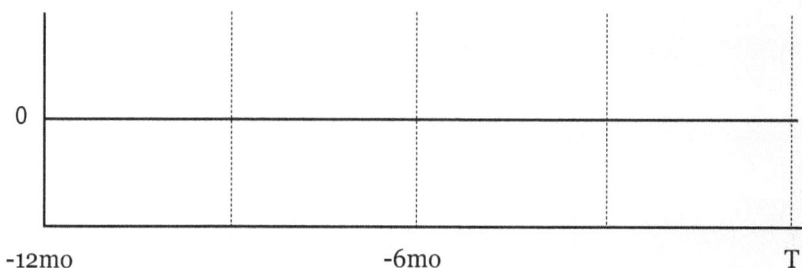

0

-12mo                              -6mo                                        T

## quote/financial highlights

Stock Price: _____
EPS: _____
P/E: _____
Market Cap: _____
Div (Yield): _____
Debt/Equity: _____
EPS Growth: Pos _____ Neg _____

## quote/financial highlights

EBIT:        Pos _____ Neg _____
Assets:      Pos _____ Neg _____
LT Debt:     Pos _____ Neg _____

## value price

EPS*10:      _____
EPS*15:      _____
Book/Share: _____

## key ratios

| | Company | Industry |
|---|---|---|
| SG: Sales | _____ | _____ |
| G: Income | _____ | _____ |
| P: Price/Sales | _____ | _____ |
| P: Price/Book | _____ | _____ |
| P: Price/CF | _____ | _____ |
| M: Net | _____ | _____ |
| I: ROE | _____ | _____ |
| I: ROA | _____ | _____ |
| I: ROC | _____ | _____ |

## personal call

| price | bargain | fair | high | crazy | decision | buy | wait | ignore |
|---|---|---|---|---|---|---|---|---|

# Stock Tracker

Personal Investment Journal
by bookmark™

company .................................................................................................

industry ........................................... industry leader ...................................

## key ratios: 10 yr comparisons

P/E: _____ > _____
P/S: _____ > _____
P/B: _____ > _____
Net Profit: _____ > _____
Book/Share: _____ > _____
ROE: _____ > _____
ROA: _____ > _____

## analyst ratings

| Strong Buy | | Mod Buy |
|---|---|---|
| | Hold | |
| Strong Sell | | Mod Sell |
| Buy | Sell | |
| Insiders | | |

## sec filings (10K/10Q)

CEO: Name _____ Years _____ Prior _____
CFO: Name _____ Years _____ Prior _____
Rational: _____ Moat Size: _____
New Products or Acquisitions: _____
_____
Competitive Advantage: _____
_____
_____
Profit Engine: _____
_____

## research

Company Web Site: _____
Wikipedia.org: _____
Google News: _____
CNBC.com: _____
Fortune.com: _____
BusinessWeek.com: _____

# Stock Tracker

Personal Investment Journal
by bookmark™ [pro]

company ............................................................... symbol .......... date ................

attention trigger ..........................................................................................

..........................................................................................

## graph (1 year)

0 ─────────────────────────────────────

-12mo                      -6mo                                    T

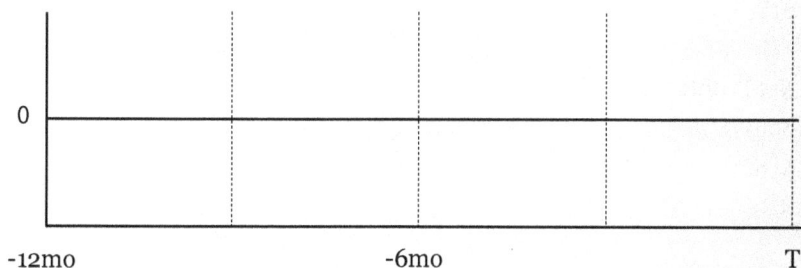

## quote/financial highlights

Stock Price: _____
EPS: _____
P/E: _____
Market Cap: _____
Div (Yield): _____
Debt/Equity: _____
EPS Growth: Pos _____ Neg _____

## quote/financial highlights

EBIT:     Pos _____ Neg _____
Assets:   Pos _____ Neg _____
LT Debt:  Pos _____ Neg _____

## value price

EPS*10:      _____
EPS*15:      _____
Book/Share:  _____

## key ratios

| | Company | Industry |
|---|---|---|
| SG: Sales | _____ | _____ |
| G: Income | _____ | _____ |
| P: Price/Sales | _____ | _____ |
| P: Price/Book | _____ | _____ |
| P: Price/CF | _____ | _____ |
| M: Net | _____ | _____ |
| I: ROE | _____ | _____ |
| I: ROA | _____ | _____ |
| I: ROC | _____ | _____ |

## personal call

price | bargain | fair | high | crazy      decision | buy | wait | ignore

# Stock Tracker

Personal Investment Journal
by pro bookmark™

company .........................................................................................................................

industry ......................................... industry leader ...........................................

## key ratios: 10 yr comparisons

P/E:          _____ > _____
P/S:          _____ > _____
P/B:          _____ > _____
Net Profit:   _____ > _____
Book/Share:   _____ > _____
ROE:          _____ > _____
ROA:          _____ > _____

## analyst ratings

| Strong Buy | | | Mod Buy |
| Hold | | |
| Strong Sell | | | Mod Sell |
| | Buy | Sell | |
| Insiders | | | |

## sec filings (10K/10Q)

CEO: Name _____ Years _____ Prior _____

CFO: Name _____ Years _____ Prior _____

Rational: _____ Moat Size: _____

New Products or Acquisitions: _____

_____

Competitive Advantage: _____

_____

_____

Profit Engine: _____

_____

## research

Company Web Site: _____

Wikipedia.org:    _____

Google News:      _____

CNBC.com:         _____

Fortune.com:      _____

BusinessWeek.com: _____

# Stocks of Interest

1 ...................................................................................................................................................

...................................................................................................................................................

2 ...................................................................................................................................................

...................................................................................................................................................

3 ...................................................................................................................................................

...................................................................................................................................................

4 ...................................................................................................................................................

...................................................................................................................................................

5 ...................................................................................................................................................

...................................................................................................................................................

6 ...................................................................................................................................................

...................................................................................................................................................

7 ...................................................................................................................................................

...................................................................................................................................................

8 ...................................................................................................................................................

...................................................................................................................................................

9 ...................................................................................................................................................

...................................................................................................................................................

10 ...................................................................................................................................................

...................................................................................................................................................

11 ...................................................................................................................................................

...................................................................................................................................................

12 ...................................................................................................................................................

...................................................................................................................................................

# Stocks of Interest

13 ..................................................................................................................

14 ..................................................................................................................

15 ..................................................................................................................

16 ..................................................................................................................

17 ..................................................................................................................

18 ..................................................................................................................

19 ..................................................................................................................

20 ..................................................................................................................

21 ..................................................................................................................

22 ..................................................................................................................

23 ..................................................................................................................

24 ..................................................................................................................

www.ingramcontent.com/pod-product-compliance
Lightning Source LLC
Chambersburg PA
CBHW021112210326
41598CB00017B/1421